WHERE THE *Spirit* OF THE LORD IS...

WHERE THE

Spirit

OF THE LORD IS...

JIM MCGUIGGAN

HOWARD
PUBLISHING CO.

Our purpose at Howard Publishing is to:

- *Increase faith* in the hearts of growing Christians
- *Inspire holiness* in the lives of believers
- *Instill hope* in the hearts of struggling people everywhere

Because He's coming again!

Where the Spirit of the Lord Is . . . © 1999 by Jim McGuiggan
All rights reserved. Printed in the United States of America
Published by Howard Publishing Co., Inc.,
3117 North 7th Street, West Monroe, Louisiana 71291-2227

99 00 01 02 03 04 05 06 07 08   10 9 8 7 6 5 4 3 2 1

Library of Congress Cataloging-in-Publication Data
McGuiggan, Jim, 1937–
    Where the spirit of the Lord is— / Jim McGuiggan.
       p. cm.
    Includes bibliographical references.
    ISBN 978-1-4516-6568-0
    1. Holy Spirit. 2. Christian life. I. Title.
BT121.2.M37   1999
231'.3—dc21   99-11020
                                           CIP

Edited by Philis Boultinghouse
Interior design by LinDee Loveland

Parker and Donna Henderson

and

Nat and Jean Cooper

who gladly pay the price to
carry the Name to the nations

Contents

CONTENTS

Contents

Introduction

Escaping the Spirit?

What the psalmist said is true: There's nowhere we can run to escape the Holy Spirit.[1] And if we unconsciously replace him with rich words like "providence" or "grace" or "faith," we make a poor trade.

W. E. Sangster observed: "Among some schools of Protestant thought, grace is the substitute for the Holy Spirit. . . . They speak of being 'fortified by grace' and 'enabled by grace' and even 'inspired by grace.' It cannot be denied; . . . we could find some justification . . . for this wide use of the word 'grace.' But even that cannot justify the virtual (if unconscious) substitution of grace for the Holy Ghost. He fortifies. He enables. He inspires."[2]

In any case, those who have been called to God's side and nurtured by that Spirit don't really want to escape him or minimize his role. To realize that the Spirit is and has been intimately involved in every phase of the self-revelation of God can only do us good and make us even more thankful.

Besides, it isn't safe to leave all talk about the Holy Spirit to those who are regarded as sensationalists. It's when we make a taboo out of a subject of central importance that it springs back with power at the first opportunity and becomes the only truth some believers want to talk about.

While I'm sure that's true, that's not the reason we want to have a rich understanding of the Spirit's person and work. Wouldn't it be wonderful if we developed a reverent but joyful intimacy with the Person who has existed in eternal holy and loving communion with the Father and the Son? How could it not be of incalculable benefit?

What follows is a very modest attempt to help us think more often, and with gratitude, about the Holy Spirit who brings us all the rich blessings of God, which are mediated to us in Jesus Christ.[3]

CHAPTER ONE

Where the Spirit of the Lord Is...

THERE IS TRANSFORMATION

A desert way,
A burning sun,
And—Saul.
A sudden light,
A heavenly voice,
And—Paul.

—Harriet Wheeler Pierson

◆

The Spirit and Mr. Hyde

In Robert Louis Stevenson's riveting *Dr. Jekyll and Mr. Hyde,* a caring doctor drinks a poison and becomes monstrous. Tragically, in real life we've seen our children drink at the wrong fountains and turn back to us with their eyes forever changed.

But where the Spirit of the Lord is we don't need to worry about the kind of transformation that will take place—it'll be from death to life and then from glory to glory.[1]

We've seen that in many lives, too, haven't we? Dead men walking with soulless eyes—changed! Happy pagans with no time for God or man—changed! Spoiled and bratty children, self-centered wimps—changed! Old men with hard, embittered spirits, as twisted in mind as in their aging bodies—changed! The self-centered and cozy, who deliberately choose to pass by neighbors or a whole world in sin and misery—changed! The smug and self-righteous, clucking their tongues and prattling on about what the world's coming to—changed! The fiercely upright, scorching the earth but avoiding costly involvement—changed! And on rare occasions, whole cities, even countries are raised out of the mire into which the whole planet would sink without a trace if God left it to itself.

Let others say the changes are simply the result of psychology, human kindness, and conditioning; fine literature, church services, new laws, or government leaders. Christians will insist that all of these and more are tools in the hands of the transforming Spirit, bringing life to the dead, passion to the indifferent, and generosity to the selfish. It is *he* who is at work convicting and sanctifying.

For the Christian, nothing less than the presence of the Spirit is enough to explain the marvelous changes worked in human lives. Call it grace; call it providence; call it the result of Bible study, practical involvement, or social ethics; call it "common grace"—call it what we will, just so we understand that in and behind any or all the instruments is the presence and work of the Spirit who seeks and finds and transforms.

There's a day coming, so say the Scriptures—without giving us any developed explanation—when this transforming work will embrace the whole creation, which presently groans in bondage. When the curse is obliterated, the creation will experience a glorious change along with the children of God. The Spirit of God is a sort of "firstfruits" of all that.[2]

Where he is present there is a change—from glory to glory!

The Lord has delivered Jacob
and redeemed him from a foe
too strong for him.

—Jeremiah 31:11 REB

✦

Of Pigs and Ancient Magic

Homer tells us that Aeëtes, the baleful king of Colchis, had a sister called Circe, a goddess who had no love for humans. After Odysseus and his crew had fought their way into the peace of a harbor, more than twenty of his men went on to the Island of Dawn to investigate. They made their way through the forest of Circe and approached her palace. They heard Circe playing the harp and looked in; she smiled and invited them in to eat. How pleased they were to be invited, and what a fine meal she fed them. But as they ate the drugged food, she hit them on their shoulders with her wand, and they changed into grunting, feverish swine.[1]

THERE IS TRANSFORMATION

"I didn't believe the story, of course," said one Christian gentleman, "until one evening when I was passing a group of young men on a street corner. I heard enough of the lascivious story being told, and I saw the leers, the flushed faces, the glistening eyes, and the muttered wickedness, and I knew I had wandered into the garden of Circe. The spell was working before my very eyes. These humans were changing into swine."

And so it is, feeding on what has been poisoned, we surrender ourselves to a spell that cheapens and coarsens us, making animals of us in our passions and the way we indulge them. We need someone wise enough and strong enough to deliver us from the curse, because in our sinfully weakened state and in a society like ours, we aren't able to do it alone.

But it's more than wisdom and strength that's needed. We need someone who *cares* greatly if we cheapen ourselves. Because she was malicious, it didn't matter to Circe that the humans were turned into animals that roamed her forests or pigs to be herded into sties. But it matters to the Holy Spirit. He seeks our sanctification because he cannot bear to see us continue in our shame. Those who don't care for us will shrug at our dishonor or give up on us before too long, especially if their wisdom isn't heeded or recognized.

Hosea, who speaks more tenderly of the love of God for his people than any other prophet, also speaks more trenchantly against the corruption of the people. He pictures God as a loving husband/father, driven to distraction by the bentness of his wife/son. The husband who paces up and down the floor, rehearsing the treachery of the wife, cannot cease to love her—doesn't want to cease to love her. The father who laments over his son's wild and reckless ways knows that the sinful boy is destroying himself, but the loving father can't turn away. "How can I give you up, Israel? How can I abandon you?"[2]

Simply reflecting on God's patience sometimes makes me tired. Sometimes, when I'm already weary and thoughts of his loving kindness come to my mind, I wonder why he doesn't just wash his hands of us all and create a world where he hears nothing but praise and sees nothing but glad-hearted obedience.

But I know better. For even I have learned enough about him to know he *cannot* abandon us, *cannot* give up on us, because it is not in him to *want* to give up on us. The often repeated words of the famous missionary Hudson Taylor come to mind: "Before I had children I knew God wouldn't forget me, but now that I have children of my own I know God *can't* forget me."

Even for those who presently don't care that they bury their snouts in swill and muck, who are content to be humans with piggish ways, there is the possibility of full reclamation because God is not willing that *any* perish.[3] And since many of us have been redeemed from just such crass wickedness, we have special reason not to give up on others.

For those of us who do care about honor and fidelity but have moments of terror when we look in a mirror and see piggy eyes looking back at us—eyes greedy for favorite sins that cheapen and damn us—we're not to despair. For if the Spirit of God works for the reclamation of those who don't care, you can be sure he works for the deliverance of those who do. He loves us more than we love our sin, and there is, as people like C. S. Lewis have reminded us, an

◆

For if the Spirit of God works for the reclamation of those who don't care, you can be sure he works for the deliverance of those who do.

7

ancient "magic" at work—a magic more wonderful than Hermes' fabled flower that delivered those who were under Circe's spell. We are even now being delivered, and one day the rescue will be completed.

Another ancient myth, every bit as terrifying as the one about Circe and her evil spells, is about a young man who cast a spell upon himself. One day as he lay by a river, he leaned over to look into the water, saw his own reflection, and fell in love with himself. More precisely, he fell in love with his image. He couldn't take his eyes off the wonder of the vision, and he died adoring himself. A narcissus plant marked the spot where he died!

It might be that those who look in terror as piggy little eyes glare back at them from the mirror are in less danger than those who love the vision they have of themselves.

It'll take wonderfully strong "magic" to deliver them from so powerful a spell. It's an awful enchantment and all the more dangerous because the self-adoring have a hard time seeing themselves as self-adoring. And what's more, they aren't repulsed by what they see, so they've no wish to be rescued.

The wicked tax-man is in less danger than the righteous Pharisee.[4] The man in the ditch whose life is oozing away with his dripping blood is not nearly as wounded and robbed as the two who energetically marched past him in their "Sunday suits."[5]

Still, we're not to despair; Christ is able to break even that evil spell from which Narcissus died. We know that, because he has done it for multiplied millions of us down the years, hasn't he!

This much we know, where the Spirit of God gets his way in a human life, glory and honor result!

I will make rivers flow on barren heights,
and springs within the valleys.
I will turn the desert into pools of water,
and the parched ground into springs.
—Isaiah 41:18

◆

Nightingales in Berkeley Square

Week after long week they waited, until weeks became months and the dry, withering months became years. The land groaned, an awful burdened groan, while the wind whispered through the dust and humans shaded their eyes morning after disappointing morning, hoping, or at least wishing. "It'll be different," said the old man, "when the rain comes." But the sky was copper, and the land panted.

Just when the last of the people began to bury their hopes, someone noticed a slight breeze one morning, and before the sun went down, the breeze became a wind. Many sat through the night, listening to it as its strength increased, and by early next morning there were clouds on the horizon. Later that day the sky filled with huge, water-saturated clouds, and the downpour began. Heavy, isolated drops at first, and then the sky opened up. The earth gulped and gurgled. Old men grinned, young men laughed in joyous relief, and children kicked at the puddles in the drenched streets. Life had come!

Around the world and in a different age, a rebellious people of God trembled as the Assyrians moved across the earth like a

✦

Old men grinned, young men laughed in joyous relief, and children kicked at the puddles in the drenched streets. Life had come!

scorching-hot wind, burning and withering everything in their path. The Assyrian didn't know it, but he was on his way to do the will of God[1] and take Israel off into "utter darkness."[2]

It's this judgment by God on treacherous and unrighteous Israel that the prophet has in mind when he speaks of desolation like this: "Beat your breasts for the pleasant fields, for the fruitful vines and for the land of my people, a land overgrown with thorns and briers—yes, mourn for all houses of merriment and for this city of revelry. The fortress will be abandoned, the noisy city deserted; citadel and watchtower will become a wasteland forever, the delight of donkeys, a pasture for flocks."[3]

Forever? Or will it just feel like forever? If not forever, how long? And the prophet tells us: "Till the Spirit is poured upon us from on high, and the desert becomes a fertile field, and the fertile field seems like a forest."[4]

He turns to speak to the gleeful and vindictive hordes of oppressors, and having said to them, "Your day's coming," he again speaks to Israel of the transformation to take place on that day when the Spirit will fall on them like life-giving rain.

The desert and the parched land will be glad; the wilderness will rejoice and blossom. Like the crocus, it will burst into bloom; it will rejoice greatly and shout for joy. The glory of Lebanon will be given to it, the splendor of Carmel and Sharon; they will see the glory of the Lord, the splendor of our God. . . . Water will gush forth in the wilderness and streams in the desert. The burning sand will become a pool, the thirsty ground bubbling springs.[5]

All this when the Spirit comes!

When I was a boy, one of the songs that everyone was singing was "A Nightingale Sang in Berkeley Square." The song tells how the world becomes a lovely, startling, and unpredictable place when love enters a life. A piece of it goes like this:

I may be right, I may be wrong,
But I'm perfectly willing to swear
That when you turned and smiled at me,
A nightingale sang in Berkeley Square.[6]

One day followed another and there was no reason to expect anything better—until love arrived—and the tame, same, ho-hum world changed. Angels were eating out at the Ritz, streets were paved with stars, and nightingales were singing where nightingales are never seen. So it was to be with Israel; so it is to be with us.

All of this when the Spirit comes.

Life bursting out of the ground and climbing to the sky. Gurgling springs where there had only been burning sand. People with broken dreams learning to dream again, the weary reviving, the feeble becoming strong, the fearful becoming brave, those with dead eyes seeing visions, the mute shouting for joy, and the deaf rejoicing just to hear it.

THERE IS TRANSFORMATION

All of this not simply because temporal blessings have been restored but because God has taken them back to his heart and redeemed them. And having ransomed them, he led them with singing into Zion, with everlasting joy as a crown on their heads.

All of this when the Spirit comes!

To captive Israel comes the word from God: "Do not be afraid, O Jacob, my servant. . . . For I will pour water on the thirsty land, and streams on the dry ground; I will pour out my Spirit on your offspring, and my blessing on your descendants."[7]

Is it any wonder Christ found the masses thirsty and looking heavenward? And when he said he would give them drink, while it might have shocked them that he made such claims for himself, they knew what he was offering!

Love knows no limit to its endurance, no end to its trust,

no fading of its hope; it can outlast anything. It is, in fact,

the one thing that still stands when all else has fallen.

1 Corinthians 13:7–8 PHILLIPS

✦

Beauty and the Beast

Down the years, many thoughtful people have observed that no one can free us from our ugliness unless he or she loves us even in our ugliness. Of course, they learned that from the all-wise Lover of Humanity.

The Disney screen adaptation of Madame de Villeneuve's story, *Beauty and the Beast,* tells how a selfish and self-centered prince ruthlessly denied shelter to an old lady on a wintry night because her appearance repulsed him. When he discovers that the old woman is really a beautiful enchantress, he apologizes; but his loveless apology is rejected, and she turns him into a hideous beast. His outer appearance now reflects his inner ugliness.

THERE IS TRANSFORMATION

The horror would disappear, the curse said, if he could learn to love and be loved by someone in his ugliness. Years pass, and he falls into despair, losing all hope that anyone could ever love a beast like him.

When the Beast captures one of the villagers, the man's beautiful daughter, Belle, offers herself as a ransom to free her father. If she wants him free, the Beast insists, she must stay with him forever. Belle falters, asking him to step into the light where she can see him. She recoils in horror at the sight of him but gives her word that she'll stay.

Moved by Belle's love for her father, the Beast tries to please her, and then the desire to please her becomes something deeper. Though he's aware that his rage sometimes drives her from him,

◆

She doesn't deny his ugliness, but she comes to see beyond it.

still, it enters his mind—the wish, the half of a broken hope—that she might be the one who can cure him. But he overhears her say in a fit of temper that she wants nothing to do with him. Dismayed, he rumbles to himself, "I'm just fooling myself; she'll never see me as anything but a monster. It's hopeless."

Gaston, the handsome but vain and cruel villager who wants Belle, gathers the village and, working them into a fever, cries, "Kill the Beast!" And that's what they try to do.

But in the end, it isn't the villagers or handsome Gaston who kills the Beast; it's Belle and the love she has for him. She doesn't deny his ugliness, but she comes to see beyond it. "Love covers over a multitude" of things.[1] In loving him, she kills the inner beast, and the visible beast vanishes along with it.

Her willingness to recognize lovely things about the Beast, to see possibilities when others, repulsed and fearful of his influence

14

on their community, try to kill him—that's what saves the monster. And her commitment works wonders, for the Beast becomes a fine and honorable young prince. Love not only saved, it transformed.

Yes, yes, all very romantic, very appealing, very touching—but mere sentimentality. Is it really? Neither God nor life allows us to believe that!

The Bible is filled with descriptions of our race, and *ugly* isn't too strong a word for our state; *bestial* is not too harsh a description for our condition. And there's Someone who moves in the world seeking to save it from its handsome but starkly vain Gastons, who compare themselves too favorably with the Beast. There is One who even now moves about the earth transforming beasts into kings and queens in a royal priesthood.

It would be better to admit that we are too easily tired, too quickly impatient, too self-righteous and self-centered—better to admit that we are too "something" than to deny that love in the person of the Spirit of God is at work in the world changing individuals, churches, and nations; redeeming us from our stark and sinful ugliness.

Matthew 18 was not written to teach us how to get rid of offenders but how to win them back. The section teaches that every single person matters to God and that when we lovingly pursue the offender to bring about reconciliation, we're doing something that pleases God. The transgressor is worth the trouble! To dismiss him without a loving pursuit is to say that his life is of no consequence to us, that we wouldn't miss him, that nothing in or about him matters enough to us to motivate us to go the distance with him.[2]

It's at this point, I'm sure, that we are most unlike Christ. It isn't that we lack power—it's that our love lacks depth and so quickly reaches its limit. If we don't see quick results in transgressors—a marked change of attitude and behavior within a specified time—we consign them to the dungeon and eternal ugliness.

It doesn't seem to enter our heads that *we* might be hideously ugly as we go about our business of trying to change transgressors. We apparently think they deserve nothing better than for us to turn them into bloody and torn spectacles. It's all very holy work, don't you understand, and they should be grateful that we would even bother to save them. And if it means we have to degrade them—so be it! What do they expect? They sinned grievously, didn't they?

The good news is that the bad news isn't as bad as it might be. There are countless people who are like the Christ, who themselves have been loved into loveliness and make it part of living to do for others what was done and is being done for them.

Madame de Villeneuve was right, love can redeem beasts. Countless humans are living proof of it.

Turn to me and be saved . . .
for I am God, and there is no other.
—Isaiah 45:22

✦

The Wind of the Spirit

Many of us go through spiritually depressed periods that feel like near-death experiences. On advice, we read the rich biblical texts that have helped so many others, yet our hearts remain as cheerless and lifeless as a cold fireplace. We try all the spiritual tonics, speak to all the wise people, do all the spiritual aerobics, read all the books on the spiritual disciplines, and try the "seven sure steps" offered by the well-known authors—all to no avail. Our depression deepens, and despair begins to knock on the doors of our hearts.

These cures are supposed to work! They appear to have worked for other people and churches, why not us? That they haven't worked for us is a matter of real concern if we are serious about having a relationship with God that pleases rather than grieves him, one that involves our giving as well as receiving. But our prayers and promises—our vows, sworn in blood-red earnestness that we'd be better, speak better, do better, and think better—have all come to nothing. The vows were sincere—at least we thought they were—and they were made in agony. But when the passion cools, we feel that "the summer is gone and we are not saved." Despair or near despair sets in. And why wouldn't it? We share the poet's distress:

> Weary of passions unsubdued,
> Weary of vows in vain renewed,
> Of forms without the power,
> Of prayers, and hopes, complaints, and groans,
> My fainting soul in silence owns
> I can hold out no more.[1]

And the words of the sufferer become ours, "My God, my God, why have you forsaken me? Why are you so far from saving me, so far from the words of my groaning?"[2]

And in our hearts, they aren't words snarled in bitterness—they're weary and disappointed rather than angry, because with our track record we can blame no one but ourselves. Still . . . still . . . we were hoping that God in his mercy would take sides with us against ourselves and deliver us for his own name's sake.

"O my God, I cry out by day, but you do not answer, by night, and am not silent."[3] And as we complain, we're perplexed, because the God to whom we make our appeal has a reputation as a deliverer: "Yet you are enthroned as the Holy One; you are the praise of Israel. In you our fathers put their trust; they trusted and you delivered them. They cried to you and were saved; in you they trusted and were not disappointed."[4]

Wonderful stories. Salvation stories. True stories. But all the more distressing *because* they are true. Others called and were saved. We call and, instead of rescue, continue to see ourselves as worms, and our "enemies" mock us even though we throw ourselves on God for deliverance.[5]

So we lie down, exhausted, having despaired of ourselves and feeling that God must have despaired of us also. And as we lie in our silent graves with no earthly help that will make any difference, paralyzed by a crushing hopelessness, we hear the whisper of the wind; and the word of God comes to us again through a nation that was dead in sin and beyond all human help.

As a nation they had tried everything to stave off the death they richly deserved. They paid tribute until they were broke, made treaties with foreign powers, and sent ambassadors north, south, east, and west. They fortified cities and studied the ways of war. They even tried religion—they built altars; they fasted and prayed. But there was no salvation in any of their efforts. They were all just new ways of speeding the death process, and they ended up in a national grave.[6]

◆

As we lie in our silent graves, paralyzed by a crushing hopelessness, we hear the whisper of the wind.

Their bones were more than dry; they were "very dry." And there weren't only a few of them—the valley, like one giant coffin, was choked with them. The prophet spoke, and bone came together with bone; but there was no life—only a huge ravine full of skeletons. Sinews and flesh wound themselves around the bones, but there was no life—only a mighty gorge stuffed with corpses, an eerie, silent valley of corpses! Well, not completely silent. There was the wind. The man was told to speak the word of God to the wind, and the wind became the Spirit of

God entering those lifeless figures—just as on the day of creation—and they were filled with life and stood on their feet, a mighty army. A nation alive from the dead!

And hearing their story, we're persuaded to trust again—or at least not to *not* trust again. At this very moment, we may feel a sense of fatigue and despair, but it's not the end of the story. God—and may it please him to be soon—will give us reason to rejoice as life courses through us, delivering us from one enemy after another. One day we'll assemble to worship and feel compelled to turn to fellow-worshipers and speak of our deliverance. In the strength and joy of the Spirit of God, we'll dismiss depression's view of sadder days and say with the psalmist:

> He has not despised or disdained
> the suffering of the afflicted one;
> he has not hidden his face from him
> but has listened to his cry for help.[7]

And we, as our forefathers did, will enthrone God as the Holy One and the praise of our hearts. From him will come the theme of our praise in the great assembly,[8] and *our* story will be told as one of deliverance to children not yet born, and people will trust because *we* were delivered.[9]

And what is true of individuals can be true of whole congregations, and what is true of congregations can be true of cities and nations! What is true for others can be true for you. What is true for you can be true for me. Weep if you must, and tell him your poor heart's breaking—but trust, wait, and listen for the wind!

He is able to save completely.

—Hebrews 7:25

◆

He Did It for Others;
He Can Do It for You!

The Spirit will not permit sin to have victory over those who turn to him for aid. It was the Spirit himself who led Jesus to say, "The Spirit of the Lord . . . has anointed me to preach good news to the poor. He has sent me to proclaim freedom for the prisoners and recovery of sight for the blind, to release the oppressed, to proclaim the year of the Lord's favor."[1]

Doesn't the very saying of it lift your heart? It's liberating to know that Jesus came to proclaim such a message and that he guaranteed the truth of it by his life and death and glorious exaltation.

THERE IS TRANSFORMATION

We read such promises, but continued defeats tempt us to water them down—the failures oppose the promises. We place our hope in the promises, but they don't work—or, at least, they haven't worked. We rely on them, but they say more than they deliver, make us imagine more than reality supports. So we're tempted to conclude that we somehow misunderstood and that the texts really call us to accomplish something by our own striving.

We might think that, after we read the fine print, we'll find it's like humanistic psychology that finally tells us, "It's up to you!" And we aren't up to it. Feeling this way, we avoid the texts. There's no point in reading them again. We'd just feel again the rising hope and the bitter disappointment that follows; we'd feel again the guilt that steals over us when we don't experience the victory promised. So we settle for less, and this settling for less breeds resentment and cynicism, depresses our spirits, and inclines us to sneer at others, "Yeah, yeah, we've heard all those texts before, felt all that hope before, whipped ourselves up into a lather before. But experience has cooled our brains, and we now know better. You'll agree with us by and by."

The whole experience is like a heavy stone weighing us down. It's more than conscious, it lies buried deep in our souls like a foreboding. It's a wound that remains open, and our life's blood oozes away. We're anemic and tired, too tired to bother. Too tired to want to bother.

But whatever we're tempted to think, God *did* it! He turned adulterers, effeminates, drunkards, thieves, coveters, abusers of themselves with men, revilers, extortioners—he turned them into people who were washed, made holy, and justified before God.[2] They had given themselves as hostages to sin, had paraded their evil for all to see and had prowled in the stench-filled basements of life—but God changed all that! The wind of the Spirit swept through Corinth, knocking down walls, bringing light and air to long, dark corridors and musty hallways, flinging windows open, and tearing down dust-laden curtains. People came out of the dark and into the light, rubbing their eyes and seeing a new world.

W. E. Sangster opens one of his books with this blunt sentence: "The purpose of God for man is to make him holy. Not happiness first, and holiness if possible, but holiness first and bliss as a consequence."[3]

God in Christ, and through the Holy Spirit, refuses to offer us less than moral and spiritual grandeur. The presence of the Spirit and his implacable hostility to what's evil, cheap, dishonorable, and pathetic is our assurance that for those who abide in Christ there can be nothing less than glorious Christlikeness—we will be like him!

It's true that we're continually wrestling with wickedness, but it's also true that the Spirit is our helper. "For the desires of the flesh are against the Spirit, and the desires of the Spirit are against the flesh; for these are opposed to each other, to prevent you from doing what you would."[4]

God in Christ, and through the Holy Spirit, refuses to offer us less than moral and spiritual grandeur.

This is not simply the statement of unending struggle; it has the tone of assurance. The tone isn't, "Well, it's too bad, but we're always going to be stymied by 'the flesh' because it is always at odds with the Spirit."

The passage doesn't avoid tough reality: It insists that, despite our being in Christ and despite our rejection of "the flesh," we still have an inner struggle against wickedness. But it also insists that a tougher reality exists—the Spirit within us who opposes the evil! That means we won't be swallowed up by sin, because greater is he who is in us than he who is in the world.[5]

In some ways, it's those of us who are most familiar with the Spirit's promises who are in the greatest danger. Someone said that familiarity may not breed contempt, but it takes the edge off awe. Something like this is true about rich texts and glory-filled promises that drop the jaws or widen the eyes of newcomers but provoke no more than a raised eyebrow in the old-timers who have ceased to dream.

We need to say it aloud—not only to one another but to ourselves, in front of a mirror—"God did it, so don't tell me it can't be done!"

No eye pitied you . . . to have compassion on you; but you
were thrown out into the open field, when you yourself were
loathed on the day you were born. And when I passed by
you and saw you struggling in your blood, I said to you in
your blood, "Live!" Yes, I said to you in your blood, "Live!"
—Ezekiel 16:5–6 NKJV

✦

Elephant Men

I'm one of those who struggles with excess need for approval. How that has come to be doesn't matter, but the reality of it takes a lot of the perfectly legitimate contentment out of life. Those of us in this condition are tempted to try too hard or to edit ourselves and our speech in certain ways—not good ways—to gain approval and acceptance. What's worse is that even though God accepts us completely, we are not satisfied. And that's too bad!

Having said that, it's no crime to want the approval of people. New Covenant writers are pleased to tell us of people who had the approval and good report of those around them.[1] Paul sends brief "letters" of recommendation in the Book of Romans and formal letters of approving introduction where it made good sense to do so.[2]

Still, it must be a blessed freedom to be able to enjoy approval when it comes but live without it when it doesn't. It must be grand to be able to resist the temptation to "sell ourselves" to get it.

Peter and John would have liked the Sanhedrin's backing, but when it didn't come, when instead they were threatened and told to stop preaching, they did not sell out; rather they shrugged and said, "Judge for yourselves whether it is right in God's sight to obey you rather than God. For we cannot help speaking about what we have seen and heard."[3] No sale!

When a serious crisis of confidence in Paul developed among the Corinthians,[4] Paul tried hard to regain their approval. But he was more than prepared to live without it, so he said, "I care very little if I am judged by you or by any human court."[5] When we read both letters to the Corinthians, we have reason to believe he would have said this with sadness and deep disappointment since he had labored so hard by God's grace on their behalf. But he said it nevertheless! No sale!

Christ told Paul he would deliver him from the Jews and the Gentiles to whom he was sending him.[6] That turned out to be true in more ways than one, for Paul was not bound by their opinions of him; no one counted with Paul more than his Master. The praise and approval of people can become addictive, and it takes the Spirit of God to deliver us from slavery to such a potent elixir. We need to be delivered from the people we're sent to, or we won't be able to help them.

But I suppose we've all felt the alternating emotions of anger and shame that resulted from being judged by "the wise ones"— from being gazed at, assessed, pigeon-holed, and dismissed as being without accomplishment or potential or appearance. I suppose we've all experienced the snobbish looks that say we're a nonentity, a "sheep in sheep's clothing," or "a modest little man with a lot to be modest about" (as Churchill is said to have described a fellow politician). The pain in all this goes to untold depths in vulnerable people.

I know of no *quick* cure for my condition or for those who are like me—but I know a sure one. To be loved! To be loved unashamedly and without reservation by someone—anyone! That's the beginning of the end of self-despising.

To *know* we are loved! Many of us have lived long in darkness, feeling unwanted, useless, ugly, and fit only to be abused. Then into our lives comes "a significant other" who seems to care even though we are afraid to believe they do. We are afraid that if they get to know us, the warmth will dissipate and we'll be alone again. Amazingly, the better they get to know us, the more they seem to care, and so the world turns the right way up, the sun comes out, and we come to life.

Has anyone experienced this at a deeper level than John Merrick, "the Elephant Man," who was made famous by the movie of that name? Deformed beyond description, used, and abused for years in the most hideous fashion, he was profoundly alone except for those times when with damnable cruelty people intruded into his life to gape and shove "the freak" around!

A riveting piece in the movie shows the grotesque Merrick fleeing a mob through a train station. They finally corner him in a public toilet, some gaping, some laughing, some yelling insults at him as he cries out in his pain, "I am not an animal. I am not an animal! I am a human being!" And then, completely traumatized and exhausted, he sinks to the floor and wearily says, "I am a man."

THERE IS TRANSFORMATION

Dr. Frederick Treves meets Merrick, and down below the ugliness, hidden behind the ugliness, and contrary to the testimony of the ugliness, the doctor finds a sensitive human being. Down behind the horror, Merrick begins to live again!

Then comes the visit of the beautiful and acclaimed actress, Mrs. Kendall, who sees his ugliness and recognizes it, but meets it with such sensitivity and gentleness that Merrick, for the moment, rises above it. She exchanges some lines with him from Shakespeare's *Romeo and Juliet*—he reading from the book she gave him and she quoting. When the lines conclude, she smiles and, with genuine warmth and in gentle mockery, says, "Oh, Mr. Merrick, you're not an elephant man at all."

"Oh, no?" he asks softly, afraid to agree.

"You're Romeo!" she whispers and gently kisses his supremely ugly cheek.

He can hardly believe it for joy—the wonder of it all! He is overwhelmed and can scarcely believe that her beauty could meet his ugliness and in warm embrace look beyond it. But however astonishing, it had *happened,* and life floods into his sad soul.

✦

"My life is full because I know I am loved. I have gained myself."

Not long before he dies, Merrick tells Dr. Treves, "Do not worry about me, my friend. I am happy every hour of the day. My life is full because I know I am loved. I have gained myself." And then pausing to look at the doctor, he gently says, "I could not have said that if it were not for you."[7]

David Prior called this little speech "arguably one of the best descriptions we have anywhere of the impact of the gospel on one man's life."[8]

Loved *by God?* Can it be true? If we dare to believe that profoundly astonishing fact, shackles will dissolve, link by damning link, freeing us from ourselves and our paralyzing ugliness. We'll be free from the scorn of our peers who know and despise us for our sinful weaknesses and who enjoy reminding others of them. We'll be free from them because they've been outflanked and made powerless. We'll be free from them because Christ comes to us, is gentle with us, and then holds us in a warm embrace saying, "Oh, you're not an 'elephant man' at all!"

And then we, scarcely able to believe, tremblingly say, "Oh, no? I always thought I was, and with the ugliness I know is in me, I feel as though I am. Are you sure I'm not?" He whispers back, "I'm sure! You're my beautiful child!"

Where the Spirit of the Lord is, there is the love of God.[9] And where the love of God is, we are able to come to ourselves.[10] We're able to look at the Christ—out from behind our fears, pains, and ugliness—and say, "I am happy every hour of the day. My life is full because I know I am loved. I have gained myself. I could not have said that if it were not for you."

Where the Spirit of the Lord is, there is freedom to rise in joy above an unhealthy dependence on the goodwill of others. There is freedom to say that all people "count with you, but none too much."

Blessed freedom. Blessed Spirit of Freedom!

The hour has come for the Son of Man to be glorified. I tell
you the truth, unless a kernel of wheat falls to the ground
and dies, it remains only a single seed. But if it dies, it
produces many seeds. The man who loves his life will lose it.
—John 12:23–25

✦

What Is Christ Prepared to Do?

Alison Cunningham was her name, and she was the devoted nurse of Robert Louis Stevenson, whose short life was one long illness. Edmund Gosse, his friend, described Stevenson's life as a "painful and hurrying pilgrimage." Cunningham was selflessly devoted to serving Stevenson, and Stevenson never forgot her. He adored her and praised her lavishly for her good influence on him. In a letter to her, he said, "Do not suppose that I shall ever forget those long, bitter nights, when I coughed, and coughed, and was so unhappy, and you were so patient and loving with a sick child. Indeed, Cummy, I wish that I might become a man worth talking of, if it were only that you should not have thrown away your pains."[1]

31

THERE IS TRANSFORMATION

Cunningham invested her life in the writer, and because of that kind of investment, Stevenson, after fitful starts and stops in life, described himself as coming around "like a well handled ship" with God as the helmsman.

What Alison Cunningham did for Stevenson, Christ has done and continues to do for a whole world, in every generation. But this Christ does it, not for a weak and pliant and grateful child—he does it for a rebellious planet peopled by hosts of humans who either cannot, do not, or will not gladly submit to his care or join him in his purposes.

"I came," he said, "not to rob but to rescue, not to cheat but to give, not to kill but to offer fullness of life." But can he do it? Well, perhaps not *can* he do it, but will he continue to *want* to do it when people like us can be so hard, so selfish, so indifferent, so self-serving and wimpy? Can he really be aware of what he has taken on? Will he not one day—looking at many of us in our love of ease and comfort—will he not throw up his hands and say, "I've given them my best and they're no different. They're still protecting themselves, still gorging themselves while others starve. No more! I've done enough, the job's too great even for a god!"? Will he not say that? Yes, yes, we know where all the verses are that say otherwise, but don't you sometimes look inside and then around and wonder at our colossal arrogance? Our amazing self-satisfaction? Do you never feel that our pathetic and trivial little lives must surely test his resolve? Does it never stagger you that we can put out our hands and take the gift

◆

Does it never stagger you that we can put out our hands and take the gift of himself with an assured politeness, as though someone just passed us the salt?

of himself with an assured politeness, as though someone just passed us the salt? *Why would he put up with it?*

A humiliated and discouraged Elliot Ness is alone on a bridge, gloomily looking into the water, smarting from his wounds. Jimmy Malone, an honest policeman who walks the beat because he won't say yes to bribery and corruption, checks him out, and so they meet. Later, Ness approaches him about beginning a small band of Treasury men who would clean up Chicago and deal with Capone.

After some verbal exchanges about the matter, Malone dismisses Ness's offer. The frustrated but desperate Ness presses him hard: "If you want to stay on the beat, you do that. If you'd like to come with me, I need your help. I'm asking for your help."

The policeman, clearly filled with inner tensions that are pulling him one way and the other, reflecting on the cry for help, says more to himself than to Ness, "That's the thing you fear, isn't it?" And then after more thought, he says to Ness, "I think it's more important to me to stay alive . . . thank you, no."

But he can't live with his refusal, and realizing the dangers and the need for unfailing commitment, he calls on Ness to say, "You said you wanted to get Capone . . . do you really want to get him? What are you prepared to do?" This phrase he repeats again and again during the course of the war they begin against the widespread corruption and murder.

And it's that phrase that's on his lips when, after being gunned down by Capone's killer, he lies dying on the floor of his apartment, choking with the blood in his throat. He passes crucial information to Ness and then grabs him by the coat, drags himself up until he's right in his face, and snarls with his last breath, "What . . . what . . . are you prepared to do?" He himself has given

33

all he has to give and wants to know if Ness is prepared to do the same.[2]

And some of us—thinking of all that Christ has already done and desperately disappointed at our response—some of us are heartsick at our paltry lives, so full of crabbiness, smugness, trivia, and self-service. And some of us wonder if he won't wash his hands of us, wash his hands of this whole sorry mess of a world. For we have no understanding of a love like his, and we haven't a cat-haired notion why he would bother with the best of us. Feeling all this and knowing that we won't clean ourselves up because we can't; realizing, as we reflect on the years gone by, that our redemption will not be a quick cure because we're awfully sick, we come anxiously asking the Christ, "What are you prepared to do?"

And he, knowing our fears and knowing our sins and self-doubts, assures us that he will do what it takes to get the job done, and he lies down on a cross and dies. He hasn't undertaken the task thinking it was a breeze. No, not him. He knew that the Incarnation was only the beginning and that the Cross was not the end, but he makes it clear: "I'll do what it takes!"

Then we, because there's nowhere else to go, because there's nowhere else we *want* to go, don't we sigh deep within us, "O Lord, I wish that I might become a person worth talking of, if it were only that you should not have thrown away your pains."

And he—from the cross and thinking of the whole world and not just us—with his own wounds and his long, long patience, looks us in the eye and asks, "What are you prepared to do?"

CHAPTER TWO

Where the Spirit of the Lord Is...

THERE IS GLORY FOR CHRIST

He who has nothing to say about Jesus Christ has nothing to say.

—H.S. Vigeveno

Worthy Is the Lamb

We hear the quiet breathing of the Holy Spirit on every page of holy Scripture, but when we listen to what he's whispering, there is only one name on his lips—*Jesus.*

If we pay attention to his way of working, we, too, will have only one name on our lips and one thing to say: "Worthy is the Lamb." In doing this we'll be joining a vast host of men and women down through the ages who tore from their heads whatever crowns they had gained in this life and threw them at the feet of the Lord Jesus.

When we've done all we are led by the Spirit of God to do, we'll discover that Christ has been glorified. Should it happen that people applaud us, we, without fanfare or pomposity, will direct their eyes to the Lord Christ himself.

Young Arturo Toscanini set out to become a cellist and was living out his dream until at the age of nineteen, while on tour with the orchestra in Rio de Janeiro, he was called on to fill in for the conductor. He proceeded to perform Verdi's *Aida* from memory, and the world of music discovered a genius. He is praised most for his interpretation of Verdi's work and the symphonies of Beethoven, and those who know say he could get from the musicians more than any other conductor.

On many, many occasions, when he had raised the orchestra's performance of Beethoven to heights they didn't think they could attain, the artists would rise to their feet and applaud the master, until embarrassed with the length and fervor of the tribute, he had to beg them to cease. "You must see, gentlemen," he'd say, "it isn't me; it's Beethoven."

The Spirit would ceaselessly remind us, "It isn't you; it's the Lord Christ! There is no other name, no other heart, no other face—there is only One!"

Where the Spirit of the Lord is, people are glorifying Jesus Christ.

He will bring glory to me.

—John 16:14

✦

The Spirit and Center Stage

The Spirit brings glory to Christ by refusing to put himself on center stage. Whatever the Spirit does and however he does it, it is to be understood in light of Jesus' own proclamation: "He will bring glory to me."[1]

We've all known people who were the dynamic behind whatever was going on, and while we knew they were at work, they didn't parade or proclaim their presence. They were hiding in plain sight. They did their job so well that people looked at what was being accomplished more than at the prime mover in the venture. The Spirit of God models this behavior for us.

He doesn't want first place!

THERE IS GLORY FOR CHRIST

Because there is no life without him, because we have no Christ without him, because he does so much—we're tempted to forget *why* he does what he does. The Spirit does what he does to glorify the Christ, to bring the Christ, to represent the Christ.

He never parades his own presence, even though he insists that we know he is present. And when the Spirit leads people to speak—and they cannot speak without him—they speak of the Master and not of him.[2] The Spirit suffers from no identity crisis, yet you never hear him say, "Behold me!" Rather, over and over and over again he says, "Behold him!"[3]

✦

The Spirit suffers from no identity crisis, yet you never hear him say, "Behold me!" Rather, over and over and over again he says, "Behold him!"

To say we shouldn't glorify the Spirit would be nonsense! To say we shouldn't delve into his nature and work would be sheer ignorance.[4] But one of the reasons that less has been said about the Spirit down the centuries than about the Father and Son is because the Holy Spirit has unceasingly pointed to the Father and the Son. That he himself should be praised and glorified is only proper, but it honors the Spirit when we pay attention to the focus of his work in the world.[5] He is not the focus of his own holy labors. In pointing away from himself, the Spirit is not putting himself down; he is exalting the Christ.

We shouldn't think this a matter of no consequence. If this is how the Spirit works and makes it clear to us that this is how he works, it must have a deep significance. And if the Spirit of God keeps stepping aside so that we can see the glorious Lord, what does this say of the Christ? What are we to make of the one whom the Spirit insists on putting at the center?

Shouldn't that remind us that we haven't gotten to the bottom of Jesus Christ yet? Doesn't it say that there are unfathomable and unimaginable riches in the incarnate Lord?

The old cliché says that the hardest instrument to play is second fiddle. Perhaps it isn't out of place to say that the Spirit does this with enthusiasm and love for the Son. It's obviously true—but needs to be said just the same—that the words "second fiddle" lose their meaning in a setting where competition doesn't exist. Still, how fine it is to know that the Spirit of God finds joy in working to bring glory to the Savior. While it is what we would fully expect—we were never led to expect anything else—still, it's strengthening to note the harmony of it all. It gives coherence to our own lives in community when we remember that "the divine Communion of Persons" knows nothing of envy, and when a specific one is adored, all rejoice.

I will ask the Father, and he will give you another
Counselor to be with you forever.
— John 14:16

✦

Led by the Spirit

The Spirit's work is this—nothing less than this and nothing other than this—to lead people to confess Jesus as Lord.[1] Any spirit that leads anyone to curse Jesus Christ is not the Holy Spirit. Any spirit that would call us to merely admire and praise Jesus Christ while refusing him lordship over our lives—that spirit is not the Holy Spirit.

The Spirit is pleased to be called "the Spirit of Jesus" or "the Spirit of Christ" or "the Spirit of his Son," because it is Jesus, the Christ, the Son of God with whom he is in eternal, holy fellowship and with whom he cooperates to bring salvation to a lost and demented race.

THERE IS GLORY FOR CHRIST

It's true that the Spirit brings other lives to our attention so we can have examples and models to help shape our lives, but above and beyond all, it is the life of Jesus the Christ that the Spirit ceaselessly parades. Abraham or Ruth or Jeremiah or Dorcas—and ten thousand others—will give us insights and inspiration, but no life is presented as even approaching that life which is the final model of living.

As the Spirit moved down the ages to enrich lives and invest them with moral glory, he was moving toward one life above all other lives—a life so unlike every other one that it alone is chosen as the universal model. No other image is acceptable to the Spirit of God—no image is to be stamped on the hearts and lives of humans other than the image of Jesus the Christ. When the Spirit gets his way in a life, that person finally confesses that Jesus is Lord,[2] the one and only Lord.[3]

✦

"Having the mind of the Spirit," I suspect, means learning from the way he graciously assents to whatever role befalls him.

In bringing glory to Christ while refusing center stage, the Spirit teaches us that meekness isn't a quality or virtue confined to the Savior. It is characteristic of himself.

Since he is a divine Colleague to the Son, isn't it extraordinary to read, "He will not speak on his own; he will speak only what he hears"?[4] Surely, if anyone had a right to speak without consulting anyone, it would be the Spirit of God who is known peculiarly throughout Scripture as the revealer and the voice within the prophetic voice. But no, he doesn't speak from himself. He listens, takes instruction, and does what he has been asked to do.

In those moments when we feel our "rights" are being ignored and our personhood despised, maybe the Spirit's glad response to the divine arrangement will strengthen our hearts and show things in a better, softer, and holier light.

Being "led by the Spirit" and "having the mind of the Spirit," I suspect, means learning from the way he graciously assents to whatever role befalls him. I suspect it means to be led by his example as well as his teaching.

And then we hear Christ say, "He will bring glory to me by taking from what is mine and making it known to you."[5] Christ is not reluctant to speak this way, not only because there is no arrogance or wicked pride in himself, but also because there is no envy in the Spirit. It is the Holy Spirit's joy to know that the Savior's glory is everywhere recognized.

And the Lord lavishes praise and glory on the Spirit when he commits to the Spirit's keeping those who are so dear to him.

On his robe and on his thigh he has this name written:
King of Kings and Lord of Lords.
—Revelation 19:16

◆

Jesus Is Lord!

Any spirit that creates or nurtures arrogance and self-promotion is not the Holy Spirit. The Holy Spirit takes the things of Christ and parades them. He isn't in the business of taking the things of the preacher and parading them. If the preacher is being paraded, it is by a sinister spirit and not the Spirit whose only joy is to bring obedience, praise, and adoration to his divine colleague—the Christ.

There's something ugly about cocksure ministers who speak so easily and so familiarly about the Christ or the Spirit, almost as if they were "good pals" of theirs. Occasional outbursts of verbal praise aren't enough to offset a swagger and that "Jesus-is-my-good-buddy" attitude that is so out of place.

THERE IS GLORY FOR CHRIST

I think you know the sort of thing I mean: "I was shaving the other morning, and the Holy Spirit said to me, ' . . . ' and I said, 'You've got to be kidding!' " This is impertinent but bound to produce an outburst of laughter in some quarters. It's the kind of thing that makes for a happy service in the well-chosen environment, but it's so unlike anything in the biblical witness.

The Spirit becomes too "user friendly," and the element vanishes that's essential to a balance of joy and awe, the element that's essential to a genuine but reverent lightness of heart, the element that's present when people are truly aware of who it is they're having communion with—the element of joyful astonishment. When that element is absent, the self-conscious religious entertainer and entertained are the ones being glorified.

◆

When the Spirit of God is presented by word or look or gesture as too familiar, an injury has been done to all believers, and the watching world reflects on it.

One defense for all this is that the Spirit is a Spirit of joy and wants the worshipers of God to be relaxed and happy. Thus, all the clever one-liners, the smart remarks, and the laid-back atmosphere are theologically vindicated. But it's precisely the assumption that the Spirit of joy would rejoice in the continuous, shallow wise-cracking that makes it all so objectionable. We didn't learn this from the joyful Christ,[1] from any of his joy-filled apostles,[2] or from anywhere else in the joyful Spirit's Scriptures.

When the Spirit of God, who confirms Jesus Christ as the one Lord,[3] is presented by word or look or gesture as too familiar, an injury has been done to all believers, and the watching world reflects on it.

Where the Spirit of the Lord is, Jesus Christ is Lord!

Say he's a friend, say he loves us, say he doesn't rejoice in our misery, say he wants us joyful, say, even, that he cares about our happiness—but say he's Lord! Say he's good to us, say he's kind, say he's gracious, say he heals our diseases and mends our broken hearts, say he guides and delivers us daily from our sin and shame, say he assures us in the face of threatening world powers, personal suffering, and death; but for pity's sake—in light of who he is and in light of the world's mounting miseries—don't say—choke before you dare say—something like "Jesus got me a hairdresser who does my hair just right" or "He got me a parking spot when I was pressed for time"!

Right up close to the cocksure and wisecracking preacher draped with gold, precious stones, and designer clothes is the self-centered believer who sees nothing wrong in having the Lord as a personal car-parking attendant or a divine Yellow Pages.

In the name of the Creator Spirit and in the presence of a sneering, jeering world on the one hand and a sighing, crying, and dying world on the other—whatever we profess to believe—let us confess our convictions in this light: Not only is Jesus Lord, Jesus is Lord!

God exalted him to the highest place and gave him
the name that is above every name, that at the
name of Jesus every knee should bow, in heaven and
on earth and under the earth, and every tongue confess
that Jesus Christ is Lord, to the glory of God the Father.
—Philippians 2:9–11

✦

I Saw a Butterfly

We may make good servants, but we're not up to being gods.

But the lovely thing about our weaknesses, our limitations, is that they work for our good and the glory of the God we know through Christ. The light we have for the world is a light that *God* has made to shine in our hearts; it didn't rise from us. It is treasure God put in "jars of clay" to show that the power is from him and so the glory should be his.[1]

I saw a butterfly once, dancing from flower to flower, a blaze of lovely hues. I asked him, "What are you doing?" He told me, "I'm glorifying God who made me," and then he fluttered off across the field. In only a few days he would be gone!

I heard a nightingale singing her heart out one day, and I crept up to watch her as she performed on a branch for the whole wide world. "And what are you doing?" I asked her. She paused in her song long enough to say, "I'm glorifying God who made me." I walked away pleased, but sad that in a little while she'd be gone.

In Thailand one evening I saw the sun, a huge ball of various shades of orange, brilliant but not harsh, hanging in the darkening sky, beaming, silent, and magnificent. "What are you doing?" I shouted to him at the top of my voice. He came within a hundred yards of me, filling the whole sky, and let me drink in the wonder of it all before blazing with gentle power, "I'm glorifying the God who made me." Silently, slowly, and majestically, he sank below the horizon and left me there in a soft, velvet darkness. Wise men say that in a million years or so, he'll be gone.

I heard myself asking, "If they're all gone, who will glorify God forever?" and I was sure I heard a voice say, "That's your job! To him be glory in the church and in Christ Jesus throughout all generations, for ever and ever! Amen."[2]

Twice, Paul makes use of the following passage from the book of Jeremiah. Twice, he brings into focus what he everywhere says—that glory belongs only to God: "Let not the wise man boast of his wisdom or the strong man boast of his strength or the rich man boast of his riches, but let him who boasts boast about this: that he understands and knows me, that I am the Lord, who exercises kindness, justice and righteousness on earth, for in these I delight."[3]

And you've met people like that, haven't you? They have little or nothing to say about anything else in life, but they're always eager to speak the name of Christ. Quiet as a mouse until someone says something about their Lord, and then they come alive, "Excuse me, did you say something about Jesus Christ? And what did you say? What was it that you wanted us to hear about him?" And with hardly a pause for breath and without waiting for a response, they rush on in that lovely way, "Wasn't it wonderful how Christ . . . ?" and "Don't you love how he . . . ?" and "I often think . . ."

When Spurgeon was asked, "How do you get and hold people's attention?" he said, "You get a can of kerosene, pour it over yourself, set light to it, and people will come to watch you burn." How right he was! In the New Testament, whenever we read of someone being "filled with the Holy Spirit,"[4] we invariably find them heralding the name of Jesus Christ in earnest joy. The Spirit has no greater joy than to see Jesus Christ proclaimed and glorified.

Lubbock Bible teacher Norman Gipson tells the story of a woman who came to the preacher after the lesson. She was well advanced in years, which often gives people an edge. She asked him, "Preacher, has anyone ever told you that you're the greatest preacher in the world?" He blushed a bit, thought it was a bit over the top, but secretly thought she had good grounds for her question. "Well, no, they never have," he said modestly. "Well then, where did you get that impression?" she asked as she walked off.

James Denney, speaking of ministers, said something like, "No man can show himself to be clever and at the same time glorify Jesus Christ." And the Holy Spirit wrote this:[5]

> Worthy is the Lamb, who was slain,
>   to receive power and wealth and wisdom and strength
>   and honor and glory and praise!

*I waited patiently for the Lord; he turned to me
and heard my cry. He lifted me out of the slimy pit,
out of the mud and mire; he set my feet on a rock
and gave me a firm place to stand.*
—Psalm 40:1–2

✦

Wistful Unbelievers

It isn't only Christ's character that seizes our imagination, it's the cause he chooses to serve. In his Father's name, he's after the world—this big, round, teeming world! He goes after it to save it, to save it from itself and for God. All the glory of his character is devoted to that single purpose, and that purpose is part of his glory.

No wonder people everywhere and in every age glorify Christ. The richness of his character and the grandeur of his life led even the self-centered Lord Byron to murmur, "If ever God was man or man was God, Jesus Christ was both." He's had a few critics here and there, of course, but they were mostly confined to his own day and his own area, and as he said himself, it's difficult for people to honor those with whom they're very familiar.[1]

Even some who couldn't see their way to trust themselves to him thought that he and the central Story connected with him were wonderful.

Take T. H. Huxley, the man who almost single-handedly made Darwin's theories take hold in Britain. A severe and vocal critic of much that he saw in religion, he still had times when he wanted to believe the message about the Christ, because it was the kind of message one could believe with a sense of fitness. Dr. Douglas Adam told this story about Professor Huxley and a friend of his:

> A friend of mine was acting on a Royal Commission of which Professor Huxley was a member. One Sunday he and the great scientist were staying in a little country town. "I suppose you are going to church," said Huxley. "Yes," replied the friend. "What if, instead, you stayed at home and talked to me of your religion?" "No," was the reply, "for I am not clever enough to refute your arguments." "But what if you simply told me of your own experience—what religion has done for you?" My friend did not go to church that morning. He stayed at home and told Huxley the story of all that Christ had been to him. And presently there were tears in the eyes of the great agnostic as he said, "I would give my right hand if I could believe that."[2]

Christ makes even unbelievers wistful!

The truth is, we were beat, and he stood up for us. We were down and out, and he came and stood by our side. We were sure the universe was dead against us, and he came to tell us that that was a malicious lie. He speaks to the worst of us as though we had souls, said Arthur Gossip. He made people believe that whatever the past had been, it wasn't the end, made them believe in themselves because he made it clear he believed in them.

And because he did, miracles happened. His strong, clean, tender voice wakened the dead and lonely. It caused a woman to leave her pots at the well and run to proclaim life to a whole town. A scarred man, fresh from his mad life among the tombs, came home and told the most amazing stories of God's goodness and mercy. In every village he went through, he brought laughter to people on street corners and new hope and resolve to men and women who turned to give life another go, saying, "God has not abandoned us! He still cares and will continue to care."

He made people believe that whatever the past had been, it wasn't the end.

And the new lives of *these* promised new life for *all.* "He did it for me!" they would say, "He can do it for you!" Isn't that what Paul expressly said? "For that very reason I was shown mercy so that in me, the worst of sinners, Christ Jesus might display his unlimited patience as an example for those who would believe on him and receive eternal life."[3] He saved me, says Paul, so nobody else will think they're beyond saving. So nobody else will think they've been forgotten.

But that's just it, isn't it? Though there are many who care little for the salvation he offers, there are hosts of people who long for such a salvation. But they feel they are fighting a losing battle with sin and life and are in despair of winning. Some have already given up, dead certain there's no way to win. Beaten too often, they remember days without number when, with hearts throbbing, they vowed vows only to see them disappear like a morning mist.

Who can help these desperate people? Who, knowing them, can speak seriously to them of salvation and life, here and hereafter?

Jesus Christ can and does! Let others whine about the "poor material" they have to work with, let church leaders complain that they can't be expected to "do a good job" when they've nothing better to work with than a community of losers. The glory of Jesus Christ is that he has no doubts about what he can and will do! In reassuring earnestness and with full confidence, he says to us, "I can save you!"

If we seriously turn ourselves over to the Christ, genuinely give him a chance to work with us, he will not only forgive us our sins, he will redeem us through and through. The proof of that is everywhere we look. Worse cases than ours have been brought to Christ, and he cleansed and made those people whole. He doesn't care how far gone we are, doesn't cautiously inquire how deeply troubled we are before he speaks his word of promise, "I can save you!"

And he will! This is the glory of Christ.

Sacrifice and offering you did not desire, but a
body you prepared for me. . . . Here I am . . .
I have come to do your will, O God.
—Hebrews 10:5, 7

✦

Shaping the Christ

The Spirit glorified the Christ by nurturing in him all that is holy and lovely.

Hebrews 9:14 says this: "How much more, then, will the blood of Christ, who *through the eternal Spirit* offered himself unblemished to God, cleanse our consciences from acts that lead to death, so that we may serve the living God!"

It was "through the eternal Spirit"[1] that Christ offered himself without blemish to God and so enabled us to serve the living God. While the Cross was the precise moment of offering, what was offered had been nurtured over a lifetime.

From Christ's very conception, the Spirit was nurturing the child who would become an unblemished sacrifice. The angel told

Mary that "the Holy Spirit"[2] would come upon her, "*so* the holy one to be born will be called the Son of God." The Holy Spirit came upon her "so"[3] that he who was born would be holy. With such nurturing from the Holy Spirit, it isn't surprising that we hear that "Jesus grew in wisdom and stature, and in favor with God and men."[4]

♦

From Christ's very conception, the Spirit was nurturing the child who would become an unblemished sacrifice.

Luke tells us that in the Christ's special period of temptation, he entered the wilderness "full of the Holy Spirit" (that is, as one whose life habitually reflected the Spirit's influence), and using an imperfect verb, he tells us that Jesus was led about by the Spirit for the forty-day period of temptation. The Spirit did not bring Jesus to the edge of the desert and then desert him. No, the Spirit accompanied Jesus during the whole trial.[5]

Even a casual reading of the Gospels shows us the deep intimacy and mutual responsiveness that existed in the relationship between Jesus of Nazareth and the Holy Spirit throughout his earthly life and ministry.

So, when the Hebrew writer says Christ offered himself without blemish to God as a sin offering "through the eternal Spirit," we're to understand that the Spirit helped prepare the Master for his crowning gift of a sinless self. And because the sinless holiness nurtured in the Master by the Spirit is the basis for his lordship, we see that the Spirit not only helped the Christ to become the Sacrifice, he helped him to become Lord.

This Savior of ours is not Lord simply because he was raised from the dead. He is Lord because he emptied himself of glory, became a servant, and surrendered himself altogether in holy love to God through the Spirit, submitting even to humiliation on a killing cross to please his Father and save a world. God could not allow such a one to remain dead! For this cause God highly exalted him and gave him a name above every name—Lord![6] It was because the Son thought so little of grasping at power or greedily holding on to it that the Father would have everyone falling at his feet and calling him Lord!

This selfless and redemptive mind-set existed prior to the Incarnation (of course!), but it was nurtured and sustained in the human life of Jesus by the sweet and holy work of the Spirit.

"As the Father has sent me, I am sending you."
And with that he breathed on them and said,
"Receive the Holy Spirit."
—John 20:21–22

✦

The World He Came to Save

It's part of Christ's glory that when he took on the task of world salvation, he knew how difficult it would be before he started. No one saw as clearly as he sin's depths and cruelty, its entrenched nature and horror, its insolence toward God, and its killing power. He saw how it wearied its victims, how it took the light out of their eyes. He noted how it fooled them into trading diamonds for dust, fooled them into mistaking real life for an opportunity to collect experiences, the way little boys collect stamps or coins or baseball cards.

He knew the history of his own Israelite nation, a history of a people who dithered and dabbled with God—shifting their fickle loyalty at every turn. He knew that his own countrymen had broken the heart of every prophet God had sent them. And he knew with a certainty that they would do the same to him, knew they would ally themselves with pagan powers to do away with him.

Yet this is the world he came to save!

Beyond the astonishing fact that he would even want to bother is the long, long patience that he'd need to accomplish it.

A prophet hinted at the cost of such an undertaking. He said it would be done, but it would be done with infinite patience, by not breaking bruised people or snuffing them out like irritating oil wicks. And would the task be a test for him? It would, but he himself would not be snuffed out or broken by the job—he'd see it through.[1]

✦

Beyond the astonishing fact that he would even want to bother with saving us is the long, long patience that he'd need to accomplish it.

Jesus took on the task, and he keeps at it! And the wondrous thing is, he does it with no sense of gloom, with no thought that it might not turn out right in the end. No, he's convinced beyond debate that the day will one day arrive—the day that the eager creation stands on its tiptoes straining to catch sight of—the day when the consummation of God's work will be revealed in the glory of his people!

While this is the heart of the wonder, it isn't all of it. For what is incredible but true is this: As he was looking at the magnitude and the difficulty of the task, he was looking for people to help him get it done. He believes in us!

"And would you?" asks Harry E. Fosdick. "Would you set out on that task with people like us?" Tell me that isn't audacious! Tell me that isn't confidence, and I'll say you haven't thought it through. To a dozen men with hardly a cent between them, without serious schooling or social graces, not a superman among them—to those men he said, "It's my Father's will to give you the kingdom!"[2]

And amazingly, here we are two thousand years later, and he's still doing it! While many of us whimper and whine about how pathetic the church, the leadership, the commitment, and the vision are, Christ soldiers on in costly triumph to that glorious cosmic victory with those very people we whine about.

And though we may try, we can't possibly imagine the magnitude of his venture. We, like Christ, attempt to help others and are scorned; we give a little help, and more is demanded of us as if it were a right; we bless, and we're cursed for our troubles. But unlike the Christ, by and by we say we've had enough! We carry the burden until we think we aren't sufficiently appreciated, then we lay it down and walk off, feeling justified in doing so.

Maybe Edward Roland Sill's poem "Opportunity" spells out the difference between us and our Lord as well as anything can.[3]

> This I beheld, or dreamed it in a dream:
> There spread a cloud of dust along a plain;
> And underneath the cloud, or in it, raged
> A furious battle, and men yelled, and swords
> Shocked upon swords and shields. A prince's banner
> Wavered, then staggered backward, hemmed by foes.
> A craven hung along the battle's edge
> And thought, "Had I a sword of keener steel—
> That blue blade that the king's son bears—but this
> Blunt thing—!" He snapt and flung if from his hand,
> And, lowering, crept away and left the field.

THERE IS GLORY FOR CHRIST

Then came the king's son, wounded, sore bestead,
And weaponless, and saw the broken sword,
Hilt-buried in the dry and trodden sand,
And ran and snatched it, and with battle-shout
Lifted afresh, he hewed his enemy down,
And saved a great cause that heroic day.

Raise your arches, O ye gates,
raise yourselves, you ancient doors!
Welcome the glorious King.
—Psalm 24:7 MOFFATT

✦

This Christ Is King!

The glory of Christ is not simply in the beauty of his character or the meekness and love in his heart. This Jesus Christ is King! Paul's message was not simply that Christ was Lord if people would let him into their hearts. No, Christ was King whether or not people would receive it. However patient and long-suffering this Lord is, he is indeed the Lord! "The one you crucified," said Peter, "is the very one God made Lord of all."[1]

Philippi, like San Francisco, was created because gold was found there. Philip of Macedon used the city to further his military might, which his son Alexander used to conquer the world. The city was still influential some three centuries later when Brutus and Cassius fought and lost to Octavian and Mark

Antony in a war where at least three fought to make their names great. Brutus, the noblest of the four, died cursing Rome's enemies by the same river where Lydia prayed.

When Octavian gave the city of Philippi colony status and made its inhabitants citizens of Rome, he carved his name as conqueror on theater stages, proclaimed it on numerous arches, and chiseled it into the walls of the citadel's temples and administration buildings. And, of course, there were the rituals of divine honors paid to Octavian and his successors. "Caesar is Lord!" boomed out from every billboard. "You are a privileged colony of Rome and citizens of the world power!" is what they told the Philippians—and weren't the citizens pleased.

Years later, an itinerant preacher made his way into Philippi[2] and preached that Jesus Christ is Lord—not Caesar! He preached that he who made himself of no reputation, who wasn't in the business of making a name for himself—that he had been given a name above every name.[3]

Of course the Master is appealing and attractive, but he doesn't come groveling, cap in hand, in Uriah Heep style, wishing that we might give him a hearing. No! The message of Peter and others was more than an invitation, it was a proclamation, an announcement! They were heralding marvelous news about a newly crowned king—King Jesus.[4]

The "good tidings" on an inscription dated 9 B.C. and speaking of Octavian (also called Augustus) illustrates the point.

> The providence which has ordered the whole of our life, showing concern and zeal, has ordained the most perfect consummation for human life by giving to it Augustus, by filling him with virtue for doing the work of a benefactor among men, and by sending him, as it were a savior for us and those who come after us, to make war to

cease, to create order everywhere; . . . the birthday of the [Augustus] was the beginning for the world of the glad tidings that have come to men through him.[5]

This inscription was thought to be "good news," but the Greek word *euangelion,* which we find here and all over the New Testament, carries with it more than the notion of pleasing news, it's a proclamation or announcement of joy-bringing news[6] This inscription isn't inviting the people to accept the emperor if they feel like it, it declares a fact of life.

Paul and others were doing no less for Jesus Christ. We mustn't suppose that Jesus is wringing his hands over the state of affairs in the world, wishing, in that overly friendly way, that people would accept him. He is King of Kings and Lord of Lords, whether we will say so or not!

If we're not careful, says J. S. Stewart, we'll present a "gospel" of enjoyable fellowship and mutual benefit, and we'll have people believing that we're doing Jesus a favor by professing his name. Something we can't afford to lose will vanish from our message—an imperial note of command.

Bearing in mind that this Christ speaks not only to his own people but to the people of the world through his people, we need to sound the note that Christ is Lord.

This is important not only because it is the truth and because Jesus is worthy of it. It's important because a world that's all at sea, that doesn't know which way to go, that feels sure the chaos that now exists is all that ever will exist—a world that's sure it's going nowhere—such a world needs a Lord who will take this whole sorry mess and work harmony and right

A lost world needs to know that someone's in charge, someone who can be trusted to make all things right.

all the wrongs. It needs to know that someone's in charge, someone who can be trusted to make all things right. In Jesus Christ, we have such a one, and we need to present him in that light!

If we present a merely friendly Christ, it makes it more difficult to believe that he would give tough marching orders. If he's presented in no other terms than as "a friend," we begin to expect better treatment than everyone else. Though he's our friend, he never ceases to be our Lord and King, and that is part of his glory.[7]

We give thanks to you, O God, we give thanks to you!
We proclaim how great you are and tell of the
wonderful things you have done.
—Psalm 75:1 TEV

◆

Every Hair on My Head

The Christ we know is a Christ who was shaped, motivated, and empowered by the Holy Spirit. Jesus tells us that he came to our world to proclaim good news to the poor, freedom to the prisoners, recovery of sight for the blind, and release for the oppressed. And the reason he came to do all this was because he was *anointed with the Holy Spirit.*[1] Peter summarized the Master's life in similar terms: He said Jesus went about doing good and healing all that were oppressed by the devil because he had been *anointed with the Holy Spirit.*[2]

Jesus was always setting people free, always saving somebody, always giving new life and healing to others, always soothing fears and challenging defeated souls to rise up and try again, always giving people back their self-respect. People down the ages have discovered he's still doing all this, so is it any wonder that multiplied millions glorify him?

But he did what he did at great cost! There was truth in the jeering words of those around the cross who said, "He saved others, he can't save himself!" But he thought that was a price worth paying. How he must have loved it when the man hanging beside him turned to him for salvation and life. Even at the point of his death, he was still saving others.

✦

He did what he did at great cost!

We glorify Christ because his character is light-years beyond everyone. We praise him for his teaching, we thrill at his miracles, smile at and feel the rebuke of his stories, are pleased when he makes lepers fresh and new, rejoice when he lifts the fallen and gets them going again, and cheer when he calls shy women out of the shadows into the warmth of his protective presence. Without minimizing any of that, we will remember him and praise him above all for what he has done with our sins.

For Christ can do more than talk about them, more than condemn them, more than see them, analyze, or oppose them. He can forgive and obliterate them! He can defeat and ruin them. He can outflank and fool them, he can damn and bury them. It is the glory of Christ that he came to save us, and he does it!

Famous hymnist and nonconformist minister Philip Doddridge heard that an Irishman named Connell was sentenced to death at Northhampton in 1741. At great personal expense and much trouble, Doddridge investigated the whole matter. He found proof positive that Connell was innocent, that he couldn't have committed the crime because he was 120 miles away when it took place. But it was all for nothing, and the innocent man was to be hung.

They asked Connell if he had a final request, and he did. He wanted the procession to the gallows to stop for a moment in front of Doddridge's house so that he could kneel there and offer a blessing on the man who had tried so valiantly to save him.

When the procession halted, he cried out in a strong, clear voice, "Dr. Doddridge, every hair of my head thanks you; every drop of my blood thanks you! You did your best to save me, but you couldn't!"[3]

Connell's gratitude is a rebuke to us who take the salvation Christ gained for us with something like courtesy rather than passion.

It's true, of course, that we aren't always alive to the truth that he has cleansed and saved us. It's true that some of the time we seem to take our forgiveness for granted, as though someone remarked, "What a nice painting that is on your wall!" and we who have become very familiar with it replied, "Yes, it is, isn't it. I quite enjoy having that." I don't suppose we can be expected to live every moment spellbound that we are indeed reconciled to God in Jesus Christ.

But it's also true that there remains a steady glow of thankfulness that it's so, and it's true that every now and then the truth of it makes our eyes go big and round. And in adoration and humble gratitude we want to borrow Connell's words and say, "Dear Lord, every hair on my head thanks you, every drop of my blood and thought of my heart thanks you for coming to find and save me!"

CHAPTER THREE

Where the

Spirit of the

Lord Is...

THERE IS
FREEDOM

To worship is to quicken the conscience
by the holiness of God,
to feed the mind with the truth of God,
to purge the imagination by the beauty of God,
to open the heart to the love of God,
to devote the will to the purpose of God.

—William Temple

◆

Truth and Emotions

Apostle of the Heart Set Free. That's the name of F. F. Bruce's book on Paul. We think of Paul like that, don't we? Free and champion of freedom, shouting things like, "It is for freedom that Christ has set us free. Stand firm, then, and do not let yourselves be burdened again by a yoke of slavery."[1]

And yet when you survey his life, you find that he was hounded from town to town, shipwrecked, publicly flogged, imprisoned, slandered, maligned by people he brought to Christ, and deserted by friends. He felt the pain of the shamed, bore the burden of those weak in faith, and worried if the little churches he'd begun could survive the pressures. Free? It's not the first word that comes to mind.

But when he came to Christ, he was made free—free from "the law of sin and death,"[2] from the need to justify himself to his critics, from the need to hide his dealings and motives from God or man, free to admit he was weak and inadequate for the job he was called to, and therefore free to throw himself in utter dependence on God. And he was free from the tyranny of all the harsh realities of life.

Free, but not exempt! Free, because in Christ he rose above them all. Free, because the Spirit in his life relativized all the suffering, freeing him to see them for what they were—realities, but not the final or ultimate realities, because sin, suffering, and death are all passing realities that belong to a passing world!

Paul attributed his freedom to the Spirit of the Lord who was the presence of the living Christ in his life. He was so free he was able to relinquish his freedom in a host of matters.

So when I say those who are Christ's are free from harsh realities, of course I don't mean they are exempt from suffering and loss. No, I mean these things aren't the ultimate realities—God, Christ, and the Spirit are! These things, for all their power to make us sob and protest, have no power to destroy us. By God's grace they serve to enrich, enlighten, and, sometimes, soften us, and to make us compassionate toward other poor sufferers.

And I don't mean we always *feel* liberated. God help us, he has loaded us with treasure, yet we often live as if we were paupers. I don't mean this as a criticism. People who imprison themselves when the freedom they long for is theirs—whatever else they need—don't need to be brutally criticized.

Knowing a truth intellectually is only half the battle. So what's to be done? I have no certain cure, certainly no quick cure, but I know it's important to rehearse the lovely, rich truths and promises that remain when other things change. Keep telling these truths, in all their many-sided glory, and one day, walls already cracked will crumble and fall.

For a while German occupational forces dominated much of Europe, but if you told a Belgian or a Frenchman that he was a "slave," you'd be putting your health in jeopardy. Slavery and freedom are as much a state of mind as anything else.

In the meantime, if our emotions won't willingly follow the truths that are greater than our emotions, they'll just have to be dragged behind us, burden or no burden. We're free and going to be freer!

Now that this has touched your lips,
your guilt is gone, your sin forgiven.
—Isaiah 6:7 MOFFATT

✦

Free Because Forgiven

Some of us hardly remember a time when we weren't Christians. We were good girls who grew into good women and good boys who became good men. We knew we were sinners, of course, but we weren't delivered from the depths of corruption because by God's grace we never got into them. This is a condition to praise God for, and no one should regret not having been in the thick of wickedness.

Still, growing up "good" has its dangers and drawbacks. It might promote smugness and make it hard for us to understand the struggles of others who are in hand-to-hand conflict with evil on a daily basis. And while that need not be true, it's often those who are forgiven much that love much.[1] It's this thought that led Augustine to speak of "blessed guilt."

Still, "there is no difference, for all have sinned and fall short of the glory of God."[2] What a blessing to have that burden of sin rolled away! To know it's gone, to have no doubts that it has been dealt with, decisively and permanently—that's a great freedom.

You remember, don't you, how in *Pilgrim's Progress,* Christian was filled with wonder and delight when his awful burden rolled from his shoulders, down the hill to vanish forever in the deep grave![3] We, too, have been freed—freed to serve God without looking over our shoulders to see if he's glaring at us with suppressed hostility, freed to offer ourselves as servants, and freed to accept the commission.

George Adam Smith preached a wonderful lesson, reminding us that part of God's forgiving us is God's *trusting* us.[4] I'd noticed the facts in the story of Isaiah but hadn't caught the significance of them.

The prophet Isaiah had followed the crowd into unbelief, thinking that the destiny of the nation depended on a powerful human king—in Isaiah's case, the good king Uzziah. The king dies and the prophet falls apart, but when he goes to the temple he sees the true King, sitting on a throne, exalted. The prophet is filled with horror, confesses his ruin, and blurts out his sin. Fire from the altar touches his lips, and his guilt is gone, his sin is forgiven.

But that's not all! When he hears God ask for a volunteer for a difficult mission, the prophet eagerly cries, "I'm willing. Will I do?" and God trusts him with the job.[5]

"Restore to me the joy of your salvation," said the wicked but repentant David, "then I will teach transgressors your ways. . . . Save me from bloodguilt, O God . . . and my tongue will sing of your righteousness."[6] And God forgave him, and David did what he promised—he did it for the God who *trusted* him with forgiveness.

Look, we know God wants more than the chance to pardon us; he wants richness of character and depth of life. Forgiveness is no end in itself; it calls for grateful response and commitment. This means that every experience of forgiveness is also God's expression of trust that we will serve him.

"'Surely they are my people, sons who will not be false to me'; and so he became their Savior."[7] Isn't that an amazing text? But they did prove false, again and again, and still he forgave them, still he trusted them, and the token of his forgiveness was that he did indeed trust them again. "In his love and mercy he redeemed them; he lifted them up and carried them all the days of old."[8]

♦

Every experience of forgiveness is also God's expression of trust that we will serve him.

Captain Mendoza was an evil, cruel man, a slaver, murderer, a person without conscience, a predator on defenseless tribes who lived high in the mountains. A terrible experience brought him to his senses, and he offered himself as part of a mission to the very people he had enslaved and butchered, a people who had every reason to fear and hate and want him dead.

The mission group made the long and very difficult climb into the high mountains, fording dangerous rivers, scrambling up cliff faces, and slogging their way through mud in the cold and rain. It was difficult for everyone, but it was especially difficult for Mendoza, who insisted on carrying his armor and weapons—his tools of malice and greed. This his soul demanded of him. His companions offered help, but he would have none of it. The crimes were his, so the burden was his.

Exhausted and panting, he finally made it to a high plateau where his companions were waiting for him. It was then he saw the leading men of the people he had so viciously mistreated for so long. Lying prostrate in the mud and mist, the heavy burden still slung around his neck, he watched as the chief drew his knife and stood over him. Fully expecting, without protest, and feeling that he deserved the death that was coming to him, imagine his astonishment when his enemy cut the rope that tied him to his burden and rolled it over the cliff to be seen no more.

Forgiven in spite of everything! His heart melted in the warmth of their generosity and trust, and the tears that were locked inside him began to flow even as he smiled at the wonder of it all.[9]

O Lord Jesus, who came to forgive us all and to tell us that you trust us in spite of everything, do forgive us and do, by your gracious Spirit, help us to live up to that trust. Amen.

No wonder we do not lose heart! . . .
Our troubles are slight and short-lived, and
their outcome is an eternal glory
which far outweighs them.
—2 Corinthians 4:16–17 REB

✦

Free from Meaningless Pain

The woman was sobbing to her aunt that she could hardly bear the nasty disposition of her husband. "He has me so jittery," she said, "that the weight is just falling off me." The sympathetic aunt said, "Well, why don't you leave him?" Tearfully, the girl responded, "Oh, I'm going to leave him, all right. As soon as he gets me down to 110 pounds, I'm out this door."

She was making her pain serve a useful purpose, but that isn't easy to do. Didn't John Bunyan tell us that on sunny days even Giant Despair became depressed? Bad theology and harsh realities can sink us into a gloom that's deeper than depression. Even good theology isn't enough to keep dark days from bullying their way into our hearts.

Still, it has to be said, there is liberty where the Spirit of God is. We've felt it in our own lives—for all their ups and downs. We've seen the delirious joy in the lives of some fine suffering souls and watched as their contagion spread to their family and beyond. They aren't just "putting it on"; they really do experience joy in pain. Their place in God and their faith in Christ make heartache serve a profound purpose—they aren't merely victims! I know there are many who don't experience this, and I don't have any quick cure for them. I only know from my own tiny life and from the lives of great sufferers down the years that heartache doesn't have the last word—and that is profoundly assuring!

Who knows why some experience this joy while others struggle so. Life situations help to explain some of it, but of those who share the same hard lives, some can't be made gloomy while others can't be made to smile—and I don't know why.

It was a great sufferer who looked it all right in the eye and said, "For we conduct our lives on the basis of faith, not the appearance of things."[1] So when disease and death, injustice and loneliness come screaming, insisting that we're fooling ourselves, we won't have it! Millions down the years have seen hard times and even now we all know people who look at life's tough challenge, walk around it, examine it in detail, nod now and then, and grunt, confessing the seriousness of it all before saying, "Yeah, that's . . . that's tough okay. But with the Spirit of God in my life I can handle it, so let's get on with it!" These people aren't victims—they're free to control these things rather than to be controlled by them.

This ministry of the Spirit[2] is God's merciful gift, so Paul says he doesn't lose heart:[3] "Though outwardly we are wasting away, yet inwardly we are being renewed day by day. For our light and momentary troubles are achieving for us an eternal glory that far outweighs them all. So we fix our eyes not on what is seen, but on what is unseen. For what is seen is temporary, but what is unseen is eternal."[4]

Is this true? Is that much glory ahead? If so, we should be able to see painful realities in a different light. Those who must have unbroken pleasure and prosperity in order to sustain faith can only look at pain and wilt! Those whose only gospel is "success" find perplexity and dismay at devastating medical reports. When they face persecution for their faith, sobbing loneliness, unpaid and unpayable bills, thankless and heartless children, or abusive, suffocating parents, they fall apart.

We're not inviting devastation into our lives, but when it comes, who's better prepared to wrestle with it than a Christian? With sins forgiven and the Spirit abiding, what can't we face? With the past dealt with and our glorious future assured, we can afford to rejoice in tribulation. With a faith like ours, a Lord like ours, a hope like ours, surely we can face what the entire world faces every day. Of course we can! I suppose that to those who are worn out and worn down all this sounds glib—but it isn't! Millions are actually living the way I'm talking!

When Paul and tens of thousands of others looked at death sentences or the prospect of prolonged "sore years," by the Spirit of God, they saw God at work in them. Listen to this:[5]

> Praise be to the God and Father of our Lord Jesus Christ, the Father of compassion and the God of all comfort, who comforts us in all our troubles, so that we can comfort those in any trouble with the comfort we ourselves have received from God. . . . We do not want you to be uninformed, brothers, about the hardships we suffered in the province of Asia. We were under great pressure . . . so that we despaired even of life. Indeed, in our hearts we felt the sentence of death. But this happened that we

might not rely on ourselves but on God, who raises the dead. He has delivered us from such a deadly peril, and he will deliver us.

Here's realism: "We thought we were dead! Our backs were to the wall, the pressure was squeezing the life out of us, the hardships had us beat." And then what? God delivered them, and they discovered that all their pain had driven them to the end of their resources so that they would depend wholly on God. They discovered that only those who have been down at the point of death and despair know what it means to be raised from the dead!

Though we've been freed from the tyranny of appearance, we don't veil our eyes to what's going on. And we have compassion for those who hurt, because we know from personal experience what it is to suffer and experience loss. But we aren't like sweet-spirited atheist J. N. Findlay, who feared spreading his belief because of its unrelieved gloom.[6] For by the Spirit of God, we have turned to look at God in Christ, and through our tears, we see only glory. That glory is one that even now grows and grows and far outweighs any "light and momentary troubles." Having the same Spirit of faith as the ancient psalmist, we believe and therefore we speak[7]—hang the threatening realities! We'll risk the complaint that our words are glib and out of touch with the agony of the world.

✦

They discovered that all their pain had driven them to the end of their resources so that they would depend wholly on God.

Viktor Frankl defined *despair* as meaningless suffering. And it's that that followers of the Christ are delivered from—meaningless pain. They have no exemption from the ills that strike humans in a world as chaotic as ours. In their stronger, braver moments they don't want exemption, preferring for Christ's sake to share the pain common to humanity. But they've been assured that their suffering is serving the glorious purposes of God and that faith transforms suffering into the servant and makes the sufferer the master.

Because of his great love for us, God, who is rich in mercy,
made us alive with Christ even when we were dead in
transgressions—it is by grace you have been saved.
—Ephesians 2:4–5

◆

Free from Legalism

Not everything that goes under the label of "legalism" is legalism.[1] An apostle of grace said this: "Keeping God's commands is what counts,"[2] and it wasn't a legalist who exclaimed, "Oh, how I love your law! I meditate on it all day long."[3]

Legalism is an unhealthy stress, an emphasis, rather than a carefully defined position with a given number of creedal points. But it has terrible consequences. Legalism offers us a grotesque image of God, one that makes him look like a "cosmic hit man" who loves his work.

This kills the possibility of a warm devotion and relationship to God, and that, in turn, deprives sinners of the desire and motivation to obey him.

Legalism nurtures the view that God's kindness toward people hinges on their worthiness, while the gospel insists that God's kindness hinges on his own gracious character, despite the fact that humans are unworthy.

One of legalism's central weaknesses is that its god is so unlike the God and Father of our Lord Jesus Christ. The God of Jesus Christ is filled with longing to suffer for and redeem unholy and unworthy people, while the god of the legalist is a god of "dancing dogs."

This true story, as I recall it, came from Bob Brown, missionary to Central America and other places. He was waiting in his minibus for some friends when a local lady, wanting to make a little money, pleaded with him to come see her "dancing dogs." He refused at first but finally conceded. Along with his friends, he followed her to a shabby house and into the back where some dogs were penned up. They were absolutely skin and bone, starved nearly to death. The poor woman, with a piece of hard bread, enticed them to stand on their hind legs and follow her around, trying to get the bread, which was always held just beyond their reach. The poor starving things were made to think they might make it but were always kept on edge while denied what they needed and longed for most. What a joyless and cruel existence.

Legalism abuses and perverts God's law by exalting it to central place so that people miss the God of all grace who gives the law as an expression of grace! In practice, God is taken away and replaced by a code. Is there a greater tragedy than this? People so need a personal God—for all kinds of crucial reasons.

You can't smile or sit down and talk with a code; you can't pray, sing, or sigh to a code, and a code can't make you feel wanted! Codes are cold because they're impersonal—they can't be otherwise! You can't weep and ask a code for help. You can't say you're sorry to a code—and sometimes we just *must* say we're sorry to someone or our hearts will explode!

In the movie *The Princess Bride,* young Inigo Montoya's father was killed by a sinister man with six fingers on one hand. Inigo becomes a master swordsman and goes in search of justice. He rehearses for his friends what he will say when he meets the six-fingered murderer. "I will say, 'My name is Inigo Montoya. You killed my father. Prepare to die.' And then I'll kill him."

Then they meet. Inigo delivers his chillingly brief speech, the killer is no match for Montoya's mastery, and at sword point he begs for mercy.

"Offer me money," says the avenger.

"Yes."

"Power, too, promise me that."

"All I have and more."

"Offer me everything I ask for."

"Anything you want," he whimpers.

As he runs him through, Montoya hisses, "I want my father back."

In the middle of all the talk about law, the legalist steals the Father and leaves us with a gloomy judge whose justice would freeze salt water.

In the middle of all the talk about law, the legalist steals the Father and leaves us with a gloomy judge whose justice would freeze salt water. We've got to have more than that. Our hearts cry out for more, our sins won't die without more, and thankfully, the Bible everywhere offers more.

Isn't human need in this area illustrated by the story told about Rudyard Kipling? The famous little Englishman was very ill, and as he lay in bed, watched over by an attentive nurse, his lips began moving. She couldn't make out what he was saying and leaned over him. He was praying. When he opened his eyes, she apologized, saying, "I'm sorry, Mr. Kipling, I thought you wanted something." The old man said in a little boy's voice, "I do. I want my heavenly Father." Yes!

We need someone who's more than a Judge obsessed with his law and his own honor. We need a heavenly Father.

Legalists are characterized by their devotion to a God who has a profound difficulty in forgiving. A god whose face is almost always frowning, who's impatient because he's irritable, who's so concerned with his own honor that he flies into a rage the moment we sin. A god who will forgive, but only under very well-defined and exhaustively met conditions. (These conditions are well known by the legalists—apparently.)

Theirs is a god who is glad to forgive as soon as you grovel and fawn, as soon as you do gut-wrenching penance, as soon as you're a bundle of nerves and aren't likely to want to do wrong again, as soon as he sees to it that righteous brothers and sisters have paraded your shame long and far enough to "teach you a lesson," as soon as he's convinced you won't come running to him too often for pardon and help.

You can hear it in their sermons and in their writings. Not only in what they say, but in what they don't say.

In the New Testament, we have this rich outpouring, this gushing fullness of grace. But legalists don't speak of "the riches of his mercy" or "the riches of his goodness and forbearance and long-suffering" or "the riches of glory." They don't recite such phrases as "according to the riches of his grace, wherein he abounded towards us," or speak of a "God who is rich in mercy" and has a "great love for us" or of "forgiveness according to the riches of his grace."

Free from Legalism

Legalists hold to a serious devotion to God that lacks self-forgetting joy. If pressed, they'll admit that God occasionally smiles and is generous, that he "delights," as Micah says, in forgiving, or that he sings in pleasure over his redeemed, as Zephaniah tells us[4]—but that's only when pressed. In practice, their preaching and teaching is so overloaded with the speed and decisiveness of his judgment against sins that they have neither the heart nor the time for anything else. Since they think God is obsessed with our sins, they feel obliged to be the same.

And because they see God like this, they can't see his law as anything other than a "do-it-and-do-it-right-or-be-damned" list of commandments. They aren't able to see the law of God in the spirit of Psalm 119—something to exult in, something that would lead them to spin around, delirious with pleasure (like Snoopy in a Peanuts cartoon), and say, "O how I love thy law. "

It's all too serious for joy. Too many people are damned, don't you see. (Especially their own people, if we're to judge from the fact that that's who they seem to attack most.) God, you see, is more concerned about being obeyed, and precisely obeyed, than about our exulting in his grace, enjoying ourselves in his generous presence, and living the life we've been freely given.

But the devotees of grace sometimes feed the fires of legalism. I'm generalizing, of course, but we'll sing happy songs for hours and study for minutes. We'll roll in the aisles with laughter for ages but will scarcely sit still for some textual exploration. We'll talk about our felt needs for hours and complain that thirty-five minutes is too long to stay in serious contact with the biblical witness.

Much of our literature is toothless, endlessly the same, boringly banal. It nods at Scripture and then goes its own way. Texts aren't broken open, and the voice of God isn't heard—it's drowned out by our one-liners and endless tear-jerking illustrations. Kids are

95

bored stiff with and have little respect for a God who can't thunder as he did at Sinai. We've muzzled him with niceness! In doing this we make it appear that everyone who boldly stands up to speak against sin and injustice is unlike our "nice" God and, consequently, is a legalist.

Richard Niebuhr had this to say about a lot of preaching he'd heard: "We testify to a God without wrath, who brings men without sin, into a kingdom without judgment, through a Christ without a cross." That may not offend us; it must certainly offend God.

Although Niebuhr said this more than a generation ago, David Buttrick is a contemporary. He's one of the leaders in homiletics and has strong views about what's going on. He tells us that in the race for "church growth," we're turning preachers into "ecclesial entrepreneurs," because when you compete for souls in the religious marketplace, the congregation calls the shots and gets what it wants. He cites a Doonesbury cartoon in which a church-shopping young couple is appalled when the preacher used the word *sinners*. The young wife explains, "We're looking for a church that's supportive, a place where we can feel good about ourselves."[5]

Against this background, against not taking God and his word seriously, against the endless flow of self-help books that nod at Scripture and feed us a steady diet of pop-psychology and cotton candy, it's a nice change to hear a strong, clear, biblical proclamation (which is what legalists think they're offering).

Then there are those of us who talk a lot—I mean a lot—about grace, who have publicly shamed ourselves and have no more sense than to keep on blabbing about it as if it were a badge of honor.

Do you remember Helmut Thielicke's "publican's prayer"?

> I thank thee, God, that I am not so proud as this Pharisee; I am an extortioner, unjust, and an adulterer. That's the way human beings are, and that's what I am, but at least I admit it, and therefore I am a little better than the rest of the breed. I commit fornication twice a week, and at most ten percent of what I own comes from honest work. I am an honest man, O God, because I don't kid myself, I don't have any illusions about myself. Let your angels sing a hallelujah over this one sinner who is as honest as I am, honest enough to admit that he is a dirty dog and not hide it beneath his robes like these lying Philistines the Pharisees.[6]

This kind of sick pride in honesty would drive a "good liberal" to legalism. It becomes us who are forever talking about grace to be blameless (not sinless, I didn't say sinless!). And should it be that we sin grievously, our response should be humble contrition rather than bold rehearsal. Nothing curls the lip of a legalist quicker than a grace-talker who makes a spectacle of himself and seems to be bragging about it or one who's savage and graceless in his dealing with others. (I'll say nothing about legalistic people who shame themselves also.)

But after we've said all we might say about legalism, showing that it's not the same as obeying God, explaining that it's sometimes a reaction to our foolishness—after all that, we still need to see it for what it is.

If there is legalism in us, we need to hunt it

◆

If there is legalism in us, we need to hunt it down and kill it, for it's a mad and sinister destroyer, an enemy of God and humanity.

down and kill it! Ruthlessly, without mercy or remorse, for it's a mad and sinister destroyer, an enemy of God and humanity. In every place where it is exterminated, a cry of praise should go up to God who helped us slaughter it!

In its place, we long to have, must have, cannot do without, the God and Father of the cross-bearing, sin-killing, life-bringing, and death-destroying Jesus Christ who calls us to and enables us in lives of honor.

And that's what the work of the Spirit is all about. "Therefore, there is now no condemnation for those who are in Christ Jesus, because through Christ Jesus the law of the Spirit of life set me free from the law of sin and death."[7]

Still, dyed-in-the-wool legalists are loved by God, and Christ died for love of them.

Ruth replied, "Don't urge me to leave you or to turn back
from you. Where you go I will go, and where you stay I will
stay. Your people will be my people and your God my God.
Where you die I will die, and there I will be buried."
—Ruth 1:16–17

✦

Free to Say No to Freedom

A man of the Spirit said, "Where the Spirit of the Lord is, there is freedom!"[1] You can almost hear him shout the words, can't you?

But was there ever a man so driven, so bound and compelled? His love for Christ was poured out in his heart by the Holy Spirit, and that's who led him to say, "For the love of Christ leaves us no choice."[2]

Having found freedom, having joyously embraced it and fiercely defended it against legalists and bigots, what did he do with it? In the name of Christ, he gave it away. "Though I am free and belong to no man, I make myself a slave to everyone."[3]

G. K. Chesterton could always get to the heart of things. Here's the kind of thing I mean. In talking about people who attack binding commitments, vows, and especially the marriage covenant, who say that such vows hinder love, that love mustn't be bound by things like marriage, Chesterton says,

> It is most amusing to listen to opponents of marriage on this subject. They appear to imagine that the ideal of constancy was a yoke mysteriously imposed by the devil, instead of being, as it is, a yoke imposed by lovers on themselves. They have invented a phrase that is a black-and-white contradiction in two words—"free-love"—as if a lover ever had been, or ever could be, free. It is of the nature of love to bind itself, and the institution of marriage merely paid the average man the compliment of taking him at his word.

Yes!

And that's why Paul ran halfway across the world, impatient with anyone who would hold him back, telling everyone he met that God in Jesus Christ had come to the rebellious world to make peace with it. With the love of God in his heart,[4] Paul was controlled by the Spirit and driven from home and into the misery and sewage of cities like Corinth to become a servant ambassador of his Lord. He was propelled by love!

Imagine a slave on the last night of bondage. His six years of service are up, and tomorrow he will be set free. Incredible as it may seem, he's thinking that he might refuse the offer. The next day he is to be given enough materials for a brand-new start—but his heart isn't in it. In the service of this master, a whole new life has opened up for him. New relationships, new loves, new dignity, new purposes, new hopes, new vision. No wonder he goes to bed with his mind made up to proclaim publicly, "I love my master . . . and do not want to go free."[5]

This is what Scottish preacher Hugh Mackintosh called "love's refusal," and it fits Paul's situation like a glove. "Freedom is good and Christ gives it abundantly; but freedom without Christ, freedom rather to put away Christ, is evil through and through. Freedom is sweet, but what are all its joys if to taste them we must leave our best Friend behind? Whatever we must renounce is as nothing to that which we have found in Him."[6]

A new love, a new world, life, and relationships had begun for a rising young Pharisee who had the old world at his feet. He saw the Christ, the Spirit called, and the young man traded his dust for diamonds. He was beyond leaving now. "I love my master and do not want to go free."

One of the riveting and tragic pieces of history in the Old Testament is the story of David's tempestuous relationship with his handsome but wild son Absalom. After years of undermining his father, Absalom gains the loyalty of the men of Israel, and David is forced to leave the palace. In a sad procession, the king's hand-picked troops see him and his family safely out of the city. Among the troops are six hundred Philistine warriors from Gath headed up by Ittai. David reminds Ittai that he and his men are foreigners and owe David no loyalty. He urges Ittai to go back to the city and offer his services to the new king. David's future is uncertain, he tells Ittai; so, think of your own interests. "May kindness and faithfulness be with you."

But Ittai won't hear of it. He had come to stay. He says, "As surely as the Lord lives, and as my lord the king lives, wherever my lord the king may be, whether it means life or death, there will your servant be."[7]

This is "love's refusal"!

Once in a while I like to imagine Jesus, apart from all his glory, meeting Paul along some dusty road that runs through some far-from-home hills—the young Master and the older missionary.

"Wherever my lord the king may be, whether it means life or death, there will your servant be."

"And do you ever think you made a big mistake, Paul?" I imagine the Master saying. "Ever feel you'd like to go back and carry that glorious career you had to a famous conclusion? Ever feel like you've had enough and want to call it a day?"

And I imagine Paul protesting, "Oh no, Master! I know I made the right choice. You've heard me preach, and you know all about the things I've written, the way I've lived my life for your sake . . . "

"Yes," Christ would say, "I know that when the adrenaline's flowing, when you're in full flight, preaching to the crowds or carried away by the excitement of the adventure—I know you wouldn't want to leave. But don't you ever get tired and wish you hadn't committed so much? Ever long for the respect of your influential peers in Jerusalem? Ever look at the tiny struggling assemblies and think it's all a waste of time? Ever listen to them devouring one another over trivial things and wish you were on another planet? In your weariness and frustration and disappointment, don't you sometimes wish you could just lay the burden down and walk away?"[8]

Wouldn't Paul look at the young Master and say, "It's true; sometimes I'm bone weary and disappointed with the response, frustrated with those for whom I've spent myself only to have them doubt my integrity. And yes, sometimes I'm angry with hucksters who take advantage of my work. There are times when I'm lonely because I've no friends around . . . and the pains and the beatings and running through the streets with mobs at my heels . . . but where would I go? Who else would love me as you do? No, my Lord, there's nowhere I'd want to go if you weren't there!"

Isn't that what he'd say?

Isn't that what you'd say?

Isn't that what many of you who live under heartbreaking conditions are saying daily?

I am poor and needy;
come quickly to me, O God.
You are my help and my deliverer;
O Lord, do not delay.
—Psalm 70:5

◆

Free from Abusive Emotions

Abusive emotions! Some of us could write a book about them: emotions that defy all explanation, that jeer at common sense, and scorn our attempts to banish them by will power; feelings that aren't content to torment us during our waking hours but continue to gnaw through the night while we try to sleep; feelings that fill our dreams with visions of failure and images that terrify; emotions that cheat us, that won't allow us to receive praise in any shape or form, that transform a compliment into one more occasion of self-doubt and an offer of friendship into another chance to suffer disappointment when the friend becomes weary of us. Abusive emotions are battery acid that eats its way through the stuff that holds us together as persons.

These feelings look on our every work with cynical eyes or a yawn; they refuse to give us the pleasure of rejoicing in some noble task well done. "Big deal!" they sneer. "In the end, what difference will it make?"

These emotions make us feel like fools because we often want to weep for no good reason; they sometimes make us doubt our sanity and always convince us that we're worthless. They shut our mouths even when we think we have something useful to say, even when we think there is something we should say. They create in us a groveling tone because we're afraid to sound too positive ("Can't have people thinking we're arrogant!") or an overly humble tone that embarrasses everyone and aggravates our self-loathing.

They perpetuate untruths that we're half afraid might be true. They slice or deaden us till we cry out to God for help, and then they mock us when the prayers bring no peace. We go around with our eyes lowered, feeling unworthy, or we go looking for a fight because we're resentful and want to prove ourselves to somebody.

They whisper the ugly lie that because we haven't yet been delivered, we never can be—the profoundly ugly lie that since God hasn't yet delivered us, he doesn't want to deliver us.

Who knows where these abusive emotions originate. Much of the time we're half afraid to find out, in case knowing would make matters worse. But however difficult it is, we must focus on the truth that the Spirit is a tireless enemy of all that shackles and blinds us. He is! He will make our pain serve his wondrous purposes while he works our healing, but he is an enemy of all that crushes the heart and narrows life. Believe it! The Master himself said: "The Spirit of the Lord is on me, because he has anointed me to preach good news to the poor. He has sent me to proclaim freedom for the prisoners and recovery of sight to the blind, to release the oppressed, to proclaim the year of the Lord's favor."[1]

It comes down to this: Either our fears are true or Christ is!

The question is not, "Can these emotions be uprooted?" The bottom line is, "Did he come to rescue us? Will he not keep his promise? Has he not shown he's able in the lives of tens of thousands? Will he leave his loved one an emotional basket case?"

♦

If we can believe he cares—if we can believe he cares no matter what is hidden down in the depths of us, that he cares regardless of our past failures, that he cares even though he knows our past, present, and future—if we can believe that, we can be healed! We will be healed! Knowing that he loves us, deeply and pro-

It comes down to this: Either our fears are true or Christ is!

foundly, is itself the sound of doom to all the twisted, rooted, and abusive emotions.[2]

In Ian Maclaren's book, *Beside the Bonnie Brier Bush,* Flora has run away from her home deep in the Highlands of Scotland. She ran to wicked London and learned what it was to be wicked. The news, making its way back to the old man, her father, breaks his heart. He'd been overly proud and too hard; now he fully realizes it and misses her, who's the light of his lonely life. Margaret, Flora's wise and loyal friend, subtly lets her know that the old man is brokenhearted, and this makes it easier for the shamed Flora to make her way home. Later, filled with joy and warmth, she says to Margaret, "It's a pity you don't have the Gaelic. It's the best of all languages for loving. There are fifty words for *darling,* and my father was calling me every one that night I came home."

Just the thought that the old man still loved her, longed for her, found it hard to live without her—that thought alone weakened her fears enough so that she could make the journey to the place where the fears were completely obliterated.

And having personal reasons for recognizing glibness when I meet it, I must tell you what my heart's conviction is, however glib it sounds. I believe that the truth of God's love for us is the beginning and end of our deliverance! I believe that that truth, turned over and over, reflected on, rejoiced in, talked about, offered thanks for—I believe that truth, applied to the heart by God's Spirit in all the lovely ways he does it, is the cure for a wounded and sick heart.

Too familiar to seem astonishing, too often regarded as "old hat," the truths told in Luke 15 are breathtaking.[3] God misses us when we're away from him, and he'll do whatever it takes to bring us home. And our coming home again fills him with radiance and joy. Is that not spellbinding—that he loves us so much in Christ—is that not spellbinding?

What drives out a strong emotion is a stronger emotion. What permanently drives out a strong emotion is a stronger emotion that makes a permanent home in us. And filled with the joyful wonder of the truth of God's love for us, the truth that in Christ he has come to free us, the abusers will weaken, wither, and die. No wonder the poet wrote:

> Jesus the very thought of Thee
> With sweetness fills my breast
> But sweeter far Thy face to see
> And in Thy presence rest.[4]

I will fear no evil,
for you are with me.
—Psalm 23:4

✦

Free from Anxiety

Seething, clamorous multitudes pushed and shoved and trampled the disciples. Enraged leaders poured out threats against them. And yet the Master said, "Do not be afraid, little flock, for your Father has been pleased to give you the kingdom."[1] Jesus warned his disciples that political powers would engineer their deaths[2] and drag them before intimidating councils,[3] and yet he repeatedly told them, "Don't be afraid."[4] How could he?

Jesus assured them by saying, "Your Father knows that you need food, clothes, shelter, and the like."[5] But if God won't give iron-clad assurances that they'll never be in want, what is the good of his knowing what they need?

Fear and worry won't be eliminated by God's assuring us we'll never want—he'll give no such assurance. Fear and worry are only overcome by knowing that the God who knows we need things can be trusted to act in our best interests, whatever he chooses to do!

If God won't give iron-clad assurances that we'll never be in want, what is the good of his knowing what we need?

The whole twelfth chapter of Luke is about worry. And yet, that's not all; it's about trust and about getting our priorities right. Since the Christ gave them the power of the Spirit, whose very presence announced the downfall of Satan,[6] what *wouldn't* he give them?

Even in the face of clashing multitudes desperate for the kingdom of God and religious leaders madly anxious to control that kingdom, the little flock had no reason to fear. For it was their Father's good pleasure to give that kingdom to them—not to experts in the law but to theologically naive blue-collar workers.

And since that is true, what does he then say to them? He calls them to reckless generosity and a wise prodigality.[7] Can you believe it? Those who might be tempted to hoard the little they have because they have the jitters about the future—they are the very ones he calls to sell all and give it away for a greater treasure.

What is it that would lead Jesus to speak to his insecure, "little flock" in this way? "What will happen if I can't work? If I can't meet my bills? If I can't provide for my family? If I can't find healing of my disease?" Though it achieves nothing,[8] anxiety about such things is perfectly natural.

What in Christ's statement—"Do not be afraid, little flock, for your Father has been pleased to give you the kingdom"—what in those words to his disciples would change their view of themselves and life, enabling them to rise above something as natural as fear and worry?

Well, he spoke of "your Father." The sovereign Lord of the universe was more than the sovereign Lord; he was their Father! That must count for something. Knowing he was their Father wouldn't keep them from feeling hunger pangs and the pain of isolation, but it would mean their futures were secure. The sovereign Lord was their Father! Not only is the *future* anchored for those whose Father is God; the *present* is transformed.

Jesus also told them that it was their Father's "good pleasure" to give them the kingdom. Not that he was reluctant to do it or that he was merely *willing*, but that it "pleased" him to do so. The word used carries both the notions of God's will and his pleasure. It pleased God to elect them as kingdom heirs.[9]

If he finds pleasure in giving them a treasure rich beyond expression, it cannot be that he would withhold from them, in Scrooge-like fashion, what he gives to the birds of the air or the grass of the fields.[10] Sinful parents give their children bread and fish, and the Father of this little flock knows how to give even the Holy Spirit to those who ask of him.[11]

All this takes the anxiety out of kingdom seeking.[12] Stampeding multitudes, a fragmented nation, a brooding Rome, a fearful and power-mad leadership—none of these can keep the kingdom from them. Their Father is pleased to give it to them. To them!

And what is the guarantee that they will receive the kingdom? The Spirit who drives out demonic powers and becomes their "deposit" on the complete redemption,[13] the Spirit who makes himself known by the gifts he gives and the fruit he produces.[14]

So, who do we Christians think we are? Let the failed marriages, the money problems, the parent/child turmoils, and the lower rungs on the social ladder—let them all speak their piece.

Allow the approach of old age and death to speak; let the chilling medical report have its say; let the bedlam of life, the entrenched powers of evil, the predatory landlords and politicians make their point.

When they've all spoken and our poor hearts are fractured, let's listen for the whisper of the words the Holy Spirit has given us: "Don't be afraid, little flock, for your Father has been pleased to give you the kingdom."

Reflect on the presence of the Spirit who has been given to the people of God—of which you are one (or could be one!). Reflect on the fact that in bringing in the kingdom, the eternal Spirit swept aside invisible powers that contribute to the world's rebellion and misery. Remember that when the disciples came back from their travels, they were ecstatic that the Spirit had "wiped the floor" with the enemies of humans,[15] and even the Christ himself was filled with joy by the Holy Spirit[16] at the joy of his disciples and what that implied. There are grounds for rejoicing, even in a world with as much chaos as ours.

And that joy, which comes through the Spirit, finds its ultimate experience in all of those of whom it can be said, "Your names are written in heaven."[17]

The Father knows our vulnerability; that's why Jesus called us a "little flock." But a little flock with the eternal God as their Father—whether or not they are hungry or deprived—will go on triumphing when all the well-fed, slick-talking, nation-manipulating "players" of the world have passed away.

Where the Spirit of the Lord is, there is freedom from anxiety in this respect: *While the emotion may exist, the grounds for it have passed and are passing!* The sovereign Lord is the Lord of history and circumstances, and he is the Father of the little flock whose fears are passing.

Those who are not his children meet realities they can't control. They have no refuge, and what they fear most will come upon them. Surely, this is an inexpressibly sad situation—to go out into the dark without a Father.

Fear not, little flock, for it is your Father's good pleasure to give you the kingdom!

I will boast all the more gladly about my weaknesses, so that
Christ's power may rest on me. . . . For when
I am weak, then I am strong.
—2 Corinthians 12:9–10

✦

Free from Pretense

How young are we, do you suppose, when we begin to cover up our mistakes or to pretend we don't need help and that everything is under our control? I suppose most of us are strugglers pretending to have it all together—closet failures hiding behind the masks of correct speech and external success, bitterly disappointed with ourselves that we haven't made a better show in life but talking as though things couldn't be better. Speaking for myself, I know very little about openness and inner contentment. Ah, the bliss of not having to pretend. It must be wonderful.

But it's difficult to confess failure when we think everyone else is successful. How can we admit to weakness in areas where everyone else is strong? God help us, we make it hard for every-one around us to lay down the intolerable burden of perfection when we act as though we're right on target and expect to arrive on schedule.

Charlie Brown's friend Lucy is writing and spelling out loud as she writes, "D-e-e-r."

Charlie interrupts. "That should be d-e-a-r. In the salutation of a letter, the proper word and spelling of that word is d-e-a-r."

She goes back to writing, speaking as she goes, "Deer are beau-tiful animals found in most parts of the world . . ."

Charlie is embarrassed and splutters, "I'm sorry . . . I . . . I didn't realize you were writing about deer . . . I'm sorry . . . I apologize."

Lucy: "Well, I should hope so! It seems to me that a lot of the problems in the world are caused by people who criticize other people before they know what they're talking about."

She glares while Charlie walks off, red-faced and chastened. Then she looks at what she's written, crumples the page, throws it away, and writes, "Dear Julia . . ."

I hear a lot of talk about our need to be honest with God. I know that's important, and I know there are times when we aren't, but that's never been much of a difficulty for me. And my suspicion is that it isn't much of a difficulty for others.

It's the people around us that we hide from, isn't it? We're con-fident God can and does live with who and what we are. He's out of our league, so we don't see him as a competitor, and we don't often think of him as our enemy. We can tell him everything—what a blessing that is!

"Oh, Lord, I'm so tired of pretending that I have all the answers."

"God, I wouldn't say this to anyone else, but I'm beginning to hate these bratty kids of mine. They use me like a doormat; the sooner they leave home the better."

"These silly church members are about to do me in, Lord. Forever bickering, demanding, and criticizing. A worse group of whining humans would be hard to find."

"Ah, God, my husband's illness is wearing me down. I can't stick with it much longer. When people ask me how I'm coping, I put on a brave face and pretend it's nothing. But I'm on the verge of tears sometimes, and I'm ready to scream, 'How do I cope? How do I cope? I don't cope, you idiot! I eat my knuckles in the night until they bleed, but what can I do about it?'"

I think some ministers have a hard time here. Most of us lack charisma and mesmerizing rhetoric, so we try like Hercules to prove ourselves worthy. And we almost cope—until we go to the forums and preacher lunches, where we're blown away by the talk of numbers, programs, successes, large staffs, church growth and influence, size of salary, and the like. We hear (or overhear) about the great strides being made at "55th and Macilvenny"; we leave the lunch with a fake smile and arrive home thoroughly depressed.

We begin to think that charisma, rhetoric, and methods make the difference. When we're reminded that God must be in it somewhere, we mutter something like, "You're right; of course, you're right!" but walk off still burdened, not really convinced. The one thing we're sure of is that we mustn't say with any seriousness, "I'm not up to the job!" So we trudge on, fake smile at the ready.

When Paul scorned a mask and openly said, "I'm not up to the job. It's too much for me!" it wasn't sullen bitterness! It wasn't a "loser's whine" because his pet project had failed! It had nothing to do with burnout. It was wide-eyed amazement at the awesome nature of the ministry of the Spirit.[1] In light of the grandeur of the Spirit's ministry, it isn't surprising that many feel inadequate. No—it's amazing that *anyone* feels up to the job. This is why Paul insists that we to whom the treasure has been committed are "earthen vessels."[2] He is making it clear that the power is not in the ministers—it's in the God who commissioned us.

We're not even up to *life* without God. Speaking of the hard times, Paul says, "We were under great pressure, far beyond our ability to endure, so that we despaired even of life. Indeed, in our hearts we felt the sentence of death. But this happened that we might not rely on ourselves but on God, who raises the dead."[3] Far beyond our ability to endure, he says. We felt the sentence of death, he says. That we might not rely on ourselves but on God, he says.

Paul knew that the power was God's, but this fact was decisively made known to him when all the props were ripped away! When charisma and learning, when passion and honesty, when generosity and selflessness fell barren at his feet, he was forced to look beyond them to God. When in his heart he felt he was dead, then—and not before—he was driven to trust in the God who raised Jesus from the dead. Christ's resurrection and glory became more than truths in a theological message.

C. K. Barrett is right, "Christian discipline means, for an apostle and for the church as a whole, a progressive weakening of man's instinctive self-confidence, and of the self-despair to which this leads, and the growth of radical confidence in God."[4]

It's always possible that we'll never experience the "death sentence" in any form. It's possible, I suppose, to choose a shriveled version of involvement in the life of the Spirit—a version that generates no sense of dismay or inadequacy, a version for which we're more than adequate all by ourselves, a version that says, "It's simply a question of technique, and we'll have it worked out soon." That breezy approach might be enough to satisfy some, but it's hardly the life-and-death adventure Paul was talking about.

If we have no genuine sense of inadequacy, if we feel no need to drop the pretense, we're either in wonderful, wide-eyed spiritual shape, or we're ignoramuses and have no idea what we've gotten into.

For those of us who haven't gotten there yet, there's this assurance: One day—sooner or later, here or there—with the Spirit's help, we're going to get things into perspective, and we won't care what others think. It'll be enough for us to know that we are God's, that we're going home, and that in the meantime, we're giving it our best shot. We may not be setting the world on fire, but that won't matter anymore. We'll stop trying to keep up with the Joneses, and we'll be happy with where we are in Christ, content in that healthy way to be ourselves. We'll not feel the need to preach or write or raise a family or build a church or live a life as well as others we could name.

All things considered, it must be a blessed relief for all those who are "in over their heads" to know in their bones: "We are not competent in ourselves; our competence comes from God."[5]

CHAPTER FOUR

Where the Spirit of the Lord Is...

THERE IS LOVE

Freedom is good and Christ gives it abundantly; but freedom without Christ, freedom rather to put away Christ, is evil through and through. Freedom is sweet, but what are all its joys if to taste them we must leave our best Friend behind? Whatever we must renounce is as nothing to that which we have found in Him.

—H. R. Mackintosh

◆

The Fruit of the Spirit Is . . .

Life with God—"eternal life"—is a gift that we receive only because we have a relationship with God.[1]

And that life goes far beyond pardon. It includes pardon, but outstrips it. One of the amazing graces God eternally planned for us is that he would make us look like Jesus Christ.[2] And that's where the fruit of the Spirit "of Christ" comes in.

I suspect the day will come when not only will we be amazed that God has forgiven us, we'll be astonished at how he has so marvelously changed us.

We know it's foolish when we spend so much time lamenting over how pathetic we are, but it's hard to shake that habit when we seem so selfish and insensitive—we who have been given so much, whose Lord is as wondrous as ours, and whose mission is as grand as ours. Yet the grace of God assures us that he who created the longing for goodness within us will bring it to a lovely conclusion. He who has begun a good work in us will complete it,[3] and that Spirit who is a deposit on *what* is to be finished is also our guarantee that it *will* be finished.[4]

For Paul, the harvest of the Spirit begins with love and ends with self-control, and to compare 1 Corinthians 13 with Galatians 5:22–23 is an education. James D. G. Dunn rightly reminds us that there can be no love without gifts of service (*charismata*), but there can be *charismata* without love.[5] And as Paul makes plain, without love everything is nothing!

Both 1 Corinthians 12 and 13 and Galatians 5 link the Holy Spirit with the life of love. In Galatians the Spirit's presence in the non-Torah Christians is not only full proof of righteousness apart from Jewish nationalism, it is the one sure way that the Torah's ambition would be fulfilled.[6]

I am the Lord; that is my name!
I will not give my glory to
another or my praise to idols.

—Isaiah 42:8

✦

Where It Pleases

The Holy Spirit is at work in the world—in and out of the Church. The goodness we see, wherever we see it and in whomever we see it, is the work of the Spirit of God. We ought to be thrilled with this truth. Rather than deny there is goodness outside the Church, we ought to be thrilled that there is. God claims that goodness as his, and he will not give his glory to idols or to anything else.

It's all right to say that the world is filled with wickedness, just so long as we understand it isn't filled with wickedness. There's nothing wrong with sweeping generalizations, as long as we know they're sweeping generalizations.

Who painted the Gentile world darker than Paul in the first chapter of Romans?[1] Was anyone more of a realist? And yet, in the next two chapters, he insisted that there were Gentiles who lived in honor before God and man, in keeping with what the Jewish Torah called for.[2] He speaks to the Jewish nation from their own scriptures, saying there is no one who cares for what is right, no one who speaks the truth or knows what faithfulness is,[3] but it's clear from the very texts he quotes that righteous people are complaining about another class of people—the unrighteous.

It's true that this world of ours is crazy. We see the rape of nations, global hatred, cruel children, extortioners and drug barons, corrupt government, rat-infested tenement buildings, and broken families. But in the middle of it all, there's goodness, mesmerizing self-sacrifice, love, kindness, faithfulness, and purity that stand in stark contrast to the corruption.

There's hypocrisy, but there's sincerity; there's sly self-service, but there's open-hearted generosity; there's sinister motivation behind apparently noble behavior, but there's also genuine helpfulness. It's true that there's prudent behavior that avoids evil only to be spared the consequences; it's true there's apparent forgiveness hidden by brooding hatred; it's true there is a "forgiveness" that doesn't think evil is of any consequence. But what a needless and self-righteous view it is that says only our love is love, only our kindness is kindness, only our patience is patience, only our marital faithfulness is faithfulness, only our delight in our babies is true delight.

The wind blows where it pleases!

It's too easy for Christians to paint all non-Christians as decadent and bestial, but this is not only a misuse of biblical texts; it is a denial of what we see before our very eyes, day in and day out. What? Should we look at the sacrificing parents, the loving husbands and wives, the loving and respectful sons and daughters, the devoted brothers, sisters, and friends and call it all demonic deception?

This is not only irresponsible use of Scripture, it is Christian imperialism at its ugliest! It's graceless and obscene the way we sometimes sulk when "outsiders" do something wonderful without asking our permission or help.

Instead of being afraid to credit all this to the Spirit, we should be afraid not to! Instead of debating the reality of it, we should fall down and thank the sovereign Spirit for refusing to let the people of the world degenerate so completely that the creation would fall apart! Instead of feeling embarrassed about the richness of the character we see in non-Christians, we ought to rejoice with them and tell them who it is they have to thank for the love they have for their families, who they have to thank that they maintain their integrity under pressure on the job, who they have to thank that they don't want to run around on their spouses.

> ✦
>
> *Instead of being afraid to credit the goodness we see in non-Christians to the Spirit, we should be afraid not to!*

In the course of teaching Nicodemus that it takes more than birth into the Jewish nation to enter the approaching kingdom of God, that it takes a birth from above—a birth by the Spirit—the Master said, "The wind blows wherever it pleases."[4] The physical Jews no more controlled the kingdom than they controlled the night wind they'd hear whispering over the tops of their houses.[5] Whether it's Nicodemus or us, we have no control over the Spirit of God. And, what's more, we should not want it!

If all this creates some theological difficulties for us, then we need to work them out![6]

[Love] keeps no record of wrongs.

—1 Corinthians 13:5

◆

The Bookkeeper Is Dead

Evil temper often shows itself in outbursts of uncontrolled verbal violence. But another of its faces is sullen resentment, where the "hurt one" retreats into him- or herself and resists attempts to "talk it out." This is anger cherished and internalized. People who are regularly subjected to this often say they'd prefer to be violently cursed than to endure the isolation and the cruel, brooding silence.

And because resentful people have sufficient self-control to suppress outbursts, they are able to maintain a studied correctness toward the object of their resentment. There are no obvious barbs aimed, but there are awkward silences and an increased demand for exactness in communication. Responses are curt but just short of being rude, cool but not icy, prickly but not savage. Resentment, you see, shows itself as a slow burn, not as a raging fire. A grudge is being nurtured, and a controlled anger is making itself felt—but doing so shrewdly—so that the "victim" can't be quite sure that she or he is being targeted.

The transgressor may offer a genuine apology for the wrong done or the mistake made, and the resentful controller may accept it with the mouth and never mention it again, but the transgression is still on the "books," and the offender feels it.

✦

Resentment shows itself as a slow burn, not as a raging fire.

The sullen and resentful have added slyness to their grudge, and they tick away like a time bomb, out of reach, enjoying the confusion and uncertainty they generate, passing by passages like "Do not seek revenge or bear a grudge against one of your people"[1] without noticing or, in some cases, without caring.

And resentment so easily metamorphoses into malice! While the impulsive lack the control to plan and structure the pain they inflict, the self-control of the resentful enables them to pursue their inner burning to the hurt of their victims. The resentful one is spiritually out of control, of course, but he maintains some controlling structures and so is able to plan, rationalize, and implement the torture of his prey. The corruption grows, the poison spreads, and the pleasure deepens as the victim wilts and dies. But the resentful is a withered, shriveled soul!

The ugliest character I know in literature is Roger Chillingworth in Nathaniel Hawthorne's *The Scarlet Letter*.[2] He's a man of outward uprightness and integrity, who speaks wise words and carries himself in studied quietness, asking the right questions with no interest other than "learning the truth" (of course!) and bringing transgressors to account. In his prolonged absence, his wife, whom he had sent ahead of him, has behaved immorally; and the twisted, self-serving hypocrite refuses to identify himself to the community as her husband, because he doesn't want to share her shame.

He extorts from her an oath of silence regarding their relationship and insists on knowing who her guilty partner is. She won't say, but the cunning and resentful old wretch finally guesses and puts his victim—the young preacher—on an emotional spit, roasting him over a slow fire. Hinting here, speaking out there, undermining at this point—always under the guise of a concerned helper. Eaten with jealousy, obsessed with the sin committed against him, driven by the desire to make the pain last, he hates it when the sinner finally reveals himself. He curses with his dark, cryptlike heart the fact that his victim has finally found freedom in self-exposure and admits disappointment that he can no longer exercise control.

I confess he makes me feel afraid!

I have met him.

May have even been him.

We need to be delivered from ever becoming or continuing to be him, for it's a dark and baleful spirit that leads people to worship their integrity while they are controlled by a slow-burning malice and spite.

Better be slow to anger than a fighter,
better govern one's temper than capture a city.
—Proverbs 16:32 NEB

✦

Love Isn't Touchy

Love may lead us to be angry at times, but it won't lead us to be savage; nor will it lead us to take offense at every breath.

The world is filled with appalling cruelty, wantonness, and perversity. Unbridled desire and emotions can seize not only individuals but nations and carry us to conduct we would have earlier thought incredible. Even Christian individuals and so-called Christian nations have committed and do commit wickedness at this level.

And while the Bible doesn't ignore these extreme cruelties and gross sins, it deals more with the daily and pervasive fruits of the uncontrolled will and emotions. (These commonplace emotions are the stuff world wars and church feuds are made of.)

THERE IS LOVE

Degeneracy and perversion curl our respectable toes, and he who embezzles the hard-earned future of older people makes us hot with indignation. But explosive anger is something else. It's one of those "respectable" or "high-class" sins of which John Watson spoke so bitingly.[1]

It's so common, don't you see, and the "very best" people engage in it. Besides, everyone knows there is a time for anger, and the ill-tempered person is sure there are times when he must "speak his mind." So when we confront such people with their ill temper, "it is with an undertone of toleration" and, on occasion, with a little uncertainty.

And why not? After all, while it might be regrettable, it's hardly avoidable. So we're told. But it's more than regrettable to those who are subjected to it on a daily basis, and while we should be willing to help the ill-tempered person, the ill temper itself must not be too easily "understood." Counseling in varied forms and sometimes medical help can be tools used by the Spirit to redeem the person from constant savage outbursts that devastate families. However it's done, the sooner the enraged person gains self-control, the better for all concerned.

It isn't the Spirit who minimizes this sin, and it certainly isn't the Spirit who leads a man or woman to broadcast, with a fair degree of cheerfulness, that they have a "bit of a temper" and that they're quite willing to give "whomever" a piece of their mind. They seem to see it as a virtue rather than a low-down vice. Instead of humble confession, we're left with the impression that an evil temper adds an element of

◆

We're left with the impression that evil temper adds an element of flavor to the whole personality. This makes it difficult for people to repent.

flavor to the whole personality. This makes it difficult for people to repent of their evil temper.

It's true that a well-rounded personality must have a flash point. The man or woman who can't be angered by anything lacks something important in his or her character and is either indifferent or cowardly or something not good.

But evil temper in the form of frequent outbursts of verbal violence must be pointed out as unlike the Christ and in need of confession and curing! I'm thinking of this particularly within churches and families. What an ungodly spectacle it is to see a man with veins bulging, lips pulled back from the teeth in a snarl, yelling right into the face of a cowering woman or child. It might even be more repulsive to see a child treat parents in that way. These attackers don't need to raise a hand against their victims, because verbal violence is a terribly adequate assault.

I know this: Once a man or woman loses control of his or her temper and it becomes evil temper, ground is lost that's hard to regain. People silently take note of the spectacle and close certain doors that might never be opened again.

Then there are the touchy people. "Love is not easily angered" is improved, I think, by Phillips's "Love is not touchy."[2] Of course, we don't want to be unfeeling; there could be no love or the social life that grows out of it without feelings, but the hypersensitive are too sensitive. They are "in a chronic state of being hurt." They have no outer layer of skin and are constantly on their own minds. These unfortunate people are walking masses of exposed nerve endings and pick up on every little word that could be interpreted as a slight or a snub. Even a compliment is a source of pain, if it isn't as profuse as one given to someone else. And if the potatoes at dinner were well received, they feel the meat must have been thought little of since it was only mentioned in passing.

THERE IS LOVE

Hypersensitive people live in agony, so it's important that help be given to ease their poor hearts. But they're a real burden to those who must live constantly in their presence, walking around as if on egg shells, telling the children to be quiet or to go out to play so they won't disturb the sulking parent.

And see them in congregations! Sulking and peevish. They get up and prance out of the assembly, feeling put on because their views aren't accepted. Their very presence is a wet blanket on a bright service, and they withhold their contributions over trivial matters. Too self-centered to be reasoned with and persistent pains in the neck, they don't have the sense to know they're holding whole segments of the assembly hostage to bad temper.

What makes matters worse, in some cases, is that these sufferers think they're quite thick-skinned. It's just, as they would tell us, that they couldn't help noticing the marked change of manner, coolness, or partiality. And though, they'll tell you, they aren't the kind of people to take offense readily, they don't have the skin of a rhino. It might be humorous to the casual observer, but incessant grieving and egocentricity can drive and has driven some friends to distraction and led to the shipwreck of many marriages and lives.

C. S. Lewis fumed about this kind of behavior. I don't recall which of his books I read it in, but he's on record as saying that you can only commit the sins of murder or adultery a limited number of times, while this other cruelty, carried out by hypersensitive people, is carried on ceaselessly for years, devastating multiplied millions in each generation. We play down the destructive power of ill temper to our peril. We need to be gentled and made kind; we need self-control and courtesy to keep us from scalding lives with our corrosive evil tempers and from passing our evil on to our children and their children.

The good news is that the Spirit graciously, if not always gently, continues to plow and sow in our lives to give us mastery over the reckless and damaging emotions that smolder in us and set our world on fire.

Until that day when—by the love of the Spirit who works out our sanctification[3]—we gain complete mastery, it won't hurt us to examine ourselves and our obedience to God in this area. Many women and men have spent a big part of their lives in helping people work through these liabilities, and they'll tell you there aren't any quick or easy fixes for those entrenched in this realm. But here are a few things we can do to help:

- Take the sins of disposition as seriously as we take sins of the flesh.

- Speak plainly against them, and call one another to repentance in regard to them.

- Speak often about the joys in a home of peace and about maximizing, instead of diminishing, the joy of others.

- Try not to make a drama out of every rude or unkind word spoken by those prone to anger.

- Try to balance the legitimate expectation of courtesy with a sense of pleased astonishment that, in a world like this, kindness and courtesy exist at all. However much we expect them, they're lovely visitors to our lives.

- Courageously confront the tyrants in our homes and elsewhere, and call them to repentance in the name of the Lord.

- Continue to believe, however difficult that is, that

these angry people need to be rescued and are worth rescuing.

- Trust that God can and will see us through all our trouble; trust that he will not abandon us and even now watches over us.

[Love] always protects, always trusts,
always hopes, always perseveres.
—1 Corinthians 13:7

✦

Love Protects

I'm certain that we need to dream of better days for ourselves, that we need to visualize better selves for the future. Dreaming is not escapism, for dreams cherished affect our future by affecting the present. More importantly, perhaps, dreams are visualized prayers and hopes, and as such, are the work of the Spirit of God. They're where we're heading, where we want to head.

But we don't only dream of holier lives for ourselves—that would be a "selfish" holiness. We want this for others as well, even when the reality that faces us is far from the ideal. This is the fruit of the Spirit: that we pursue not only our own holiness but theirs, that we refuse to give up on them as we refuse to give up on ourselves. Their fate is connected to ours. If God isn't able to bring freedom to others who struggle against sin, he won't be able to do it for us! Do you hear me? If he isn't adequate for them, he isn't adequate for us.

But because God is God and because the Spirit enables us, we look at the stubborn and wicked realities of life and continue to hope. We're no less realistic than Abraham, who looked at the incongruity of the promise of many descendants, his barren wife, and his own worn-out body and, against all hope, believed.[1]

In the meantime, while we can't make choices for others and can't decide for them to follow Christ, we can ask God's help to make us the kind of people who would bring others to Christ and who would protect the strugglers who are in Christ.

In 1 Corinthians 13:7, many versions say "love bears" all things—and this may be correct. A number of others, including the New International Version, give us "love protects." The word used speaks of "covering" as, for example, a roof covers and so protects. Arndt and Gingrich think "cover over in silence" might be the best rendering in this passage, though "bear" is possible.[2] They go in Moffatt's direction: "always slow to expose."

Matthew gives us some guidance in how to deal with transgressors: The *motive* is always to gain the brother or sister. They are worth the trouble. The *method* is "go and show him his fault, *just between the two of you.* If he listens to you, you have won your brother over."[3]

I've italicized a phrase in the preceding scripture that seems to me to be ignored much too often. I've sinned in ignoring it myself (and repent of it!) and have been sinned against in this matter— along with countless others. Love is in the *redeeming* business, which is why transgressors must be called to repent; but it is also in the *protecting* business, which is why it is "slow to expose" and why it follows the Master's instructions about keeping it between the offender and yourself before bringing anyone else into it.

I'm not suggesting that Matthew gives us an exhaustive set of instructions on the matter of dealing with offenses, but I am suggesting that the Spirit didn't write that so we could ignore it and feel justified in doing so.

A number of years ago, T. W. Stewart tells us, someone who was prominent in English public life, at the height of his career, brought himself to shame and imprisonment. When they were taking him into the court for trial, handcuffed between two policemen, one of his acquaintances waited in the corridor just so the shamed man could have a supportive face among the gaping crowd. At the appropriate moment, he stepped forward and raised his hat to the prisoner. Years later, the guilty man wrote: "I store that act in the treasure-house of my heart. The memory of that little, lovely, silent act of love has unsealed for me all the wells of pity, and brought me out of bitterness."[4]

✦

Love is in the protecting business, which is why it is "slow to expose" the offenses of another.

Those of us who've shamed ourselves and been publicly punished for it have no complaint about the justice of the punishment. But in addition to the pain of the shame, there is the pain of being shunned by fellow sinners, who guard their own reputations by distancing themselves from us. Job, anything but a wimp, protested against this kind of thing.[5] What this nameless man did for Stewart's prisoner changes the world! It not only redeems the guilty from bitterness; it makes us want to be like him. That is, to be like Jesus!

I am convinced that neither death nor life, neither
angels nor demons, neither the present nor the future,
nor any powers, neither height nor depth, nor anything
else in all creation, will be able to separate us from the
love of God that is in Christ Jesus our Lord.
—Romans 8:38–39

◆

God's Bundle and Ours

Christians try, in the grace and power of the Spirit, to let love and their love for God be the motivating center of their lives.[1] But, of course, it doesn't begin with them; it begins with God, for we love him because he first loved us.[2] So we claim that the love of God for humanity is the soil out of which all that is generous and kind and strong and good takes it rise.

Critics waste no time jeering at such a faith and point to the tragedies of life: "Are you people blind? Don't you see what's going on in the world? How can you say God loves humanity when you can see, or should be able to see, the absurdity of it all. In spite of the chaos, you trot off to your little praise gatherings and mouth the same silly songs, blissfully unaware that you're completely out of touch with reality."

I don't think so! I don't think the Church needs lectures on the reality of pain and loss. Do they think Christians are exempt from loss? Have we not buried our own? Watched our own die in agony? Seen our own marriages fall apart and our families endure purgatory? Christians bear loneliness and heartache, weep in the night and watch helplessly while their business, built on honest toil over many years, goes under and they are left wondering.

And maybe the critics need to know that there's a poignancy attached to the Christian's loss that they can't appreciate. In some ways, it would be easier to bear loss if, like the critic, we could disbelieve. Only a severely tested believer knows that saying, "God loves you" doesn't always solve everything. Sometimes, it makes it worse, because if he loves us, then why this or why that? Surely, if he loved us, he would have prevented this or that.

No, I don't think we need lectures about realism or hard questions. Believers throughout the centuries, as the biblical record shows, have agonized and questioned. If there were no Jewish people, no Hebrew scriptures, no New Covenant church or scriptures, it would be easier to disbelieve. If there were no Jesus Christ, that would settle the matter. Yes, if there were no Jesus Christ, we'd take our tragedy and live and die in misery without questions.

But the Spirit has poured the love of God into our hearts,[3] and we're persuaded that behind all the chaos and pain, there is a heart that works for the good of us all, critics included.

We come to God with our bundle of tragedy, our leukemic child or crippled young husband, and lay it before him, lip trembling, looking for an answer—"What am I to make of this?" Or, if not for answers, at least some kind of assurance, *something* to help us make it through the awful days. Without even a hint of displeasure or disappointment, and without a word of explanation, God lays his own bundle of tragedy beside ours—our loved one and his loved one, our heartache and his, lying there side by side. And for all our heartache, there's something in that silent act of God that comforts our hearts and gives us courage. So, without an explanation, but strengthened, we thank him and get back to the business of glorious living.

Knowing that this Lord works triumph and glory in and through tragedy, as he did with his own, we have *heart* to believe what our intellect has the *grounds* for believing: that he can and is doing wonderful things with our sore trouble.

So we make it our aim to proclaim the love of God for the whole world, fully aware of the tragic stories that poor, brokenhearted people are telling. But with a sympathy born of assurance rather than despair, we lay our own stories down beside theirs and then God's story down beside ours and speak wisely and hopefully about the love of God for us all.

Without a word of explanation, God lays his own bundle of tragedy beside ours.

145

✦

Lord of All or Not Lord at All

Where the Spirit of the Lord is, people make love their aim. He will lead us to love our families and friends, even our enemies, but he will lead us first and foremost to love the God who shows himself to us in Jesus Christ. He never confuses the first commandment with the second.[1] Never!

In a day when the family is under siege, it would be easy for believers to go overboard and worship it. But the Christ went out of his way to make it clear that the family is not the prime unit before God. Again and again, in one way or another, with urgency, he made it clear that love for him is to lead us to put all our cherished relationships under his feet.[2]

Only a fool would claim that Jesus was opposed to family and friendship, but we're missing it by a mile if we think he's willing to take second place to anyone or anything. Nor will he be fooled by lip service to his supremacy, while we make his extraordinary gifts the center of our lives.

But how can we tell when we're going overboard? I'm sure there's no programmed answer—if there is, I certainly don't have it, nor have I come across it—but I'm more than certain that as we become more like the Christ, we'll find the balance. In the meantime, while we're looking for it, we'll confess this truth we hold and want to live by: Christ alone holds the central place in our hearts.

The wonder of it all is this: When we find the Master, we find ourselves, our families and friends, even our enemies, in a clearer, finer way.

Boreham somewhere tells us of a Scottish preacher who stayed at a certain inn each year as he traveled around ministering here and there. He took a liking to the daughter of the owner, a young girl who loved life but was too filled with the pleasures it held to want to give her life to Christ. But on one visit, after numerous talks about it all, she did promise to pray each night before she went to bed, "O Lord, show me myself."

When the preacher returned about a year later, he was astonished at the change in her. All the sparkle and laughter was gone. The brightness had left her eyes and a fixed gloom had come over her spirit. As they talked, she could speak of nothing but her wickedness, her trivial life and her awful need. He tried in vain to get her to throw herself on the love and mercy of God because she felt that God's love couldn't be intended for the likes of her.

He did manage to get her to promise that every night before she retired she'd pray, "O Lord, show me thyself." The following year, he saw a transformed young woman. She wasn't the roguish and frivolous girl he had first met, nor did she have that grim, dead look of the previous year. She was joyful, had a settled peace, and was overflowing with gratitude. The first prayer had kept her looking at herself; the second kept her looking at her Savior.

To look too long at anyone or anything seduces us from the center of everything. We must find him before we can find ourselves or those we love. Becoming more like him means seeing with new eyes and in new ways. That's why, for all the weaknesses in the way they do it, Christians, in their wiser, better moments say, "We would see Jesus."[3]

Even personal holiness can become an idol and personal devotion a seduction if they are pursued as ends in themselves. Where the Spirit of the Lord is, Jesus alone is Lord! Not a congregation, not a lifestyle, not a family, not a nation, not a movement—Jesus! When Jesus becomes our Lord and we are transformed into his likeness, our families, churches, and nations receive us back richer and kinder. Noble tasks and projects receive us back more useful and more enthusiastic.

The joy of the Lord is your strength.
—Nehemiah 8:10

✦

Love Rejoices

Have you ever had a boss so mean and ill-tempered that it was a misery to go to work? Then one evening you received news so wonderful that your whole outlook changed. Work became a breeze, difficulties became mere inconveniences, and you even had a genuine smile for that misery-creating boss of yours. Joy transforms us, and that has consequences for the people around us.

"Love rejoices," Paul tells us. But this doesn't mean that the joy nurtured by the Spirit is a strictly "religious" joy. No, any joy that is honorable and related to what is wholesome and fine is the work of the Spirit and is provoked by a gift of the Spirit. To rejoice in the love of a friend, the birth of a baby, the recovery from an illness, the good fortune of a neighbor, the gifts of life—to rejoice in these, this is the work of the Spirit!

Some Christians think we should convince the world that they're miserably unhappy in order to make them feel their need to come to Christ. I'm not suggesting this should never be the approach—specific cases may urge this—but as a policy, it lacks credibility, and in the light of the glory of Christ, it's an inferior approach.

We must have a gospel for those who are sad, beaten, and bewildered, but the woman who approached E. S. Jones had a question that really matters. She said, "You have a gospel for the hurting; do you have one for the happy? I have a happy home; my husband, my children love me and I love them, and we haven't any particular financial worries. Have you any gospel for me—a happy person?"[1]

Countless non-Christians rejoice in a host of blessings that God provides for them. They can't be persuaded that they find no joy in a loving family, good food, clean air and water, physical health, and pleasant social conditions. To tell them they aren't "happy" is to ask for a scornful response. When they speak to us about these blessings, rather than dismissing them, shouldn't we be saying something like, "Yes, isn't life wonderful! And isn't God good to us? And shouldn't we give him all the glory?"

Of course it's true that the joy created by these blessings will pass when the blessings pass. So? To say that joy in these is not eternal is not to say it isn't joy! Temporal joys will fade for Christians also.[2] They're sandcastles, to be built with giggling and abandon, thoroughly enjoyed but not expected to last. Though they're passing, these blessings are real and given to all creation by the Creator Spirit for us to enjoy with thanksgiving.[3]

Still, joy doesn't rise to its loveliest, most precious and most enduring, when we have the "world by the tail." No. When the disciples came back rejoicing at the demonic retreat, Christ was pleased with and for them, but he said, "However, do not rejoice that the spirits submit to you, but rejoice that your names are written in heaven."[4]

He wasn't forbidding joy over demonic defeat, he was stressing joy about something that went beyond those victories. Joy that comes as a result of things that are lovely and honorable is the work of the Spirit, but there is a hierarchy of blessings which we need to recognize. And as our hearts are transformed by the Spirit, no doubt we'll rearrange our earlier listings.

Life without any form of disablement is no small blessing, but to suffer some disablement isn't the end of the world. If God didn't want us, didn't put our name in his book of life—that would be the end of the world!

To miss the position or job we wanted most may be a great blow to us, and to go through life with some precious dreams unfulfilled will have its pain. There are some things we don't want to miss, and there are others we mustn't miss. And that's part of what the Spirit does for us; he teaches us how to dream, what kind of things to dream for, and how to go on living radiantly when we miss some of the things we had our hearts set on.

In the movie *Field of Dreams,* Ray meets up with Archie Graham, a well-loved doctor who for many years carried in his heart a lovely dream that was never fulfilled. He had come "within five minutes" of batting in a major league baseball game and had treasured for so long the dream of what he might have done and how thrilled he would have been to do it.

Ray invites him to a special place where past dreams can be fulfilled. The old doctor turns down the offer saying that the most special place in all the world was where he was—he couldn't leave now. Ray says he understands but pleads with the doctor, "Fifteen years ago, for five minutes . . . you came this close . . . I mean it would kill some men to get this close to their dream and not touch it. They'd consider it a tragedy."

The older man with quiet passion says, "Son, if I'd only gotten to be a doctor for five minutes, that would have been a tragedy."

Life is filled with joys, rich and fine and clean and good. Every one of them a gift of the Spirit. Every one of them to be received with thanksgiving and without apology, but there are joys and then there are joys. It is the highest work of the Spirit to offer to us and create within us the deep pleasure that arises from knowing that we have life with God, and that he finds joy in us.[5] Now that is joy at the highest and most durable level.

And it's not only right for us to enjoy God's blessings, it is one of God's ways to give us power to see life through in an honorable and contagious way.

One day, Ezra and his companions read the scriptures to the assembled people, and as the people listened, they began to grieve. But the leaders urged them to accept the holy day as a day of celebration rather than mourning, for, they said, "The joy of the Lord is your strength."[6]

In what way was the joy of the Lord their strength? By God's grace, grief and depression may later yield a great harvest, but they can also weaken us, make us vulnerable, and result in despair. A glad heart does the opposite. It makes us feel better about ourselves, about those around us, about the world at large. Bad things don't seem so bad, painful things don't seem so painful. We dismiss as trivia some of the things we thought were burdens when our hearts were depressed. Even major problems are easier (not easy) to handle when we're experiencing something that is lifting our hearts. The joy doesn't make the trouble disappear, but it enables us to size it up better, see it in perspective, and it gives us needed energy to work with it.

The joy of the Lord is our strength!

The joy God offered them would be good for them. It would give them strength. And since it was a strength that came from gladness, rather than from stubbornness or grimness—a buoyant strength rather than a grim slog—it would make life easier, not only for them but for everyone around them. It would be infectious.

◆

How fine it is to be around people who are carried along by the strength of joy even in the middle of sore years. Yes, there is a joyous gospel for the happy people, and when the gospel comes at us through happy people, it is even more winsome and persuasive. The Spirit of God gives us joy, and it becomes a strength. William Barclay tells us that someone asked Rufus Mosely if he thought Jesus ever laughed. He said, "I don't know, but he certainly fixed me up so I can laugh."[7]

Joy doesn't make the trouble disappear, but it enables us to size it up better and see it in perspective.

A joyful life is not only easier, but praise God, it's contagious!

Cast all your anxiety on him
because he cares for you.
—1 Peter 5:7

✦

Love and Peace of Mind

One aspect of my sinfulness is my impatience with those I perceive to be wimps. I need to balance that by assuring you that I don't brutalize them, but I do wish to confess and renounce my impatience for what it is. I know, as I'm sure you do, people who live with tough and enduring situations; so when others make a drama out of lower-level challenges, I'm afraid I often take a mental note. I know my "wimp-spotting" must always be provisional, but I've seen even gentle psychoanalysts roll their eyes at such in mock despair.

I say all that just to clear a place to stand while saying that I think people with depressed spirits get a raw deal.

We seem to forget that a broken heart is at least as painful as a broken rib, a depressed spirit as disabling as broken legs. We give sympathy, encouragement, and gifts to the physically traumatized; and ultimatums or ill-concealed lack of interest to the emotionally down who repeat their story "one more time."

We seem to forget that a broken heart is at least as painful as a broken rib, a depressed spirit as disabling as broken legs.

Even Jesus experienced intense, negative emotions: "Anguish and dismay came over him and he said to them, 'My heart is ready to break with grief.'"[1] So it's possible to be full of the Spirit and yet experience waves of "not joy" emotion.

Here's a horror story—the kind I hope is rare. A young girl asked me if I'd speak to her mother who was terribly depressed. When I went to her home, the lady wept bitterly and told me of the loss of her husband. They had loved each other so long, and then her companion had died, leaving her alone. She had walked the house at night for months, unable to sleep, wanting to talk to him, sometimes calling out for him, sometimes angry with him for leaving her, sometimes angry with God for letting it happen. For a couple of months, she'd gotten sympathy and some visits from various fellow Christians. Then the leaders came and pointed out that she hadn't been to church in the months since her husband died. They gave her an ultimatum—meet with the church or be withdrawn from! She snapped and asked them to leave. She hadn't been to an assembly since—it'd been more than a year and a half. She was frightened about what God would think but couldn't generate the inner strength needed to get out and go to church.

Whatever she'd needed by way of challenge, comfort, and

reminders of the hope the gospel brings, she hadn't needed an ultimatum! Her broken heart was as painful and as real as any compound fracture.

Depression need not be sin or even an occasion for criticism in the same way that joy need not be seen as a virtue or an occasion to praise. Everything depends on where these emotions rise from and what, by God's grace, we do with them.

Not many things are more infuriating than to have a "permanent grinner" scorn your depression as a lack of faith, when he knows nothing whatever of your life. It's possible for fear and depression to become sinful or arise out of some sinful situation, but only God can speak with certainty in these matters. Depression comes to us all.

Paul made no bones about it: He could feel beaten down when things weren't going well with the churches he'd established.[2] He saw his "anxiety" over the churches he worked with as one of the proofs of his apostleship.[3] If he didn't worry, that would say he was indifferent to their state and that, for him, would mean he hadn't been given the gospel. Morbid concern takes on the nature of sin, but worry—which is fear of loss of something precious—sometimes comes because we love deeply. Its presence isn't always sin, and its absence sometimes suggests something sinister.

Maybe we should be slow to attribute sin to the worriers and the depressed. Maybe we should do our homework on Jesus' call to people not to be anxious. Maybe we should stop sticking our grinning faces before the emotionally hurting to toothily bully them with, "Smile, God loves you." Maybe we ought to be much more modest about what we "know" about the inner workings of people.

When people tell us to pull ourselves together, they often forget that what we pull ourselves together with is broken or faulty. They're asking us to do precisely what it is we can't do at the moment.

Maybe we need to make sure we're instruments of the Spirit by making love our aim toward the hurting rather than further depressing them.

CHAPTER FIVE

Where the Spirit of the Lord Is...

THERE IS COMMUNITY

What life have you if you have not life together?
There is no life that is not in community,
And no community not lived in praise of God.

—*Harriet Wheeler Pierson*

◆

We're Something Else

Out of the uninhabitable, the Spirit created a home; and out of the chaos, he produced harmony.[1] Everything flourished, everything was in its assigned place, and life was complete and harmonious, until—until we bought into a lie: We believed we were gods. Disharmony and fragmentation were the results. God's response was a redemption that is still being carried to a grand and glorious conclusion, a conclusion even more glorious than its original creation.[2]

The New Testament makes reconciliation and peace central to the work of Jesus Christ and insists that they only take place in "one body."[3] Not only were we never meant to live alone, there is no life alone.

Nor is spiritual growth or maturity possible without community. It's together that we have access to and grow into the fullness of God.[4]

The Hebrew writer urges us: "And let us think of one another and how we can encourage one another to love and do good deeds. And let us not hold aloof from our church meetings, as some do. Let us do all we can to help one another's faith."[5]

For years his life had been filled with bitterness, suspicion, and loneliness. He'd hurt a lot of people and been hurt; he'd drunk way too much and spent most of his time existing rather than living. Then he met her. Her life was like his except for the booze. Before they knew it, they'd become close, closer than close. The world became a different place. Only weeks earlier, it had been purgatory without reprieve, but now there were friendly faces on every corner; the sun shone and work was a breeze.

In a tender moment, as they looked at one another in silence, in that lovely way that friends and lovers often do, he whispered, "You're something else!" Her gracious response was, "No, *we're* something else."

Apart they'd both been embittered, licking their wounds and cursing life. Together they brought the best out of each other. Apart they were loose cannons; together they moved in unison, finding joy in pleasing one another.

But it was more than that. It wasn't only that they brought out the best in one another, they invested each other with things the other didn't have when alone.

And it's that kind of community that we've been called to in Jesus Christ. Where the Spirit of the Lord is and gets his way, people are coming together.

How good and pleasant it is
when brothers live together in unity!
—Psalm 133:1

◆

Weeping in the Aisles

It's our destiny to be one! God has never been interested—eternally not interested—in creating us to live as independent units. No, it's stronger than that: He's earnestly and eternally passionate about our being one, about our belonging to Christ and consequently to one another! This isn't an option; it's the heart of the matter. It isn't a fringe benefit we get when we sign on; it's the purpose and creation of God—a creation that we're to treasure and, by his grace, maintain.[1]

"For in Christ Jesus you are all sons of God, through faith. For as many of you as were baptized into Christ have put on Christ. There is neither Jew nor Greek, there is neither slave nor free, there is neither male nor female; for you are all one in Christ

Jesus."[2] This is where God has been leading humanity since he first purposed creation: to a harmony and glory that would not only negate the curse that came in when we rebelled, but would outshine the glory of our original state. This new creation and glory began and is seen in the Lord Jesus Christ.

Genesis 3–11 is a record of self-assertion that began in the Garden of Eden and culminated in the plain of Shinar. We were tired of being homeless wanderers and said if God wouldn't give us a home of our own, if he wouldn't give us dignity and rest and honor, we'd create it by and for ourselves. We'd settle the land, build our own power center, make a name for ourselves, and erect a tower to our glory and godhood.

God wouldn't allow it, and he mercifully scattered us. There'd be no home without him, no name without him, no glory without him, no rest without him. Fragmented, off we went to establish numerous power centers, structures less grand than the one at Shinar, but our own just the same.[3]

The existence of the Community of the Reconciled is a protest against Sin's work of fragmenting the nations. Its existence is a visible witness of God's faithfulness to ancient promises and eternal purposes. It's a protest against all forms of elitism that set humans against humans. It isn't only a judgment against the needless splintering among believers; it blows the whistle on all that tears a world apart!

If there's a place on earth where someone can run to be free from racist, sexist, radical nationalist, or any other elitist talk, thought, attitudes, or behavior—if there is such a place, it should be the Church!

If we find it difficult to bring our emotions, speech, and thinking into line with this because of our culture or raising, we should admit it and pray to God for help to get it done. In the meantime, if our emotions aren't ready for this, they should be dragged kicking and protesting to where we're headed; our emotions are not our lord, Christ is! What fragments us is God's enemy and ours.

This came home to a group of believers at a congregational level some years ago. They were planning an outreach program in their wider community and got together at the building to pray about it. A man was called to open the period in prayer. He went to the pulpit, and the people bowed their heads. There was a long silence—too long, way too long—and finally, people began to look up to see what was going on. The leader still stood there, as if he'd begin, but then he began to shake his head. Finally, he apologized and said he couldn't lead the prayer until he got something settled.

He had an old grievance with another man in the assembly, he said, and he couldn't go on with the meeting until it was made right. The place was silent as a tomb and every eye watched as he made his way to the middle of the auditorium. He beckoned a man out of his seat and into the aisle. He whispered a long and tearful apology, and they hugged and prayed right there where they stood.

If our emotions aren't ready to dispense with elitism, they should be dragged kicking and protesting to where we're headed.

While this was going on, others got up out of their seats and found individuals they needed to talk with. Before they knew what was happening, the auditorium was filled with people, whole families, seeking each other out, softly apologizing one to another, weeping and holding one another. Others were smiling at the amazing transformation that was taking place before their eyes. Isn't that wonderful?

As I recall the conclusion of the article, the word got around in that community of what had happened, and that congregation had a more effective outreach than they could ever have hoped for.

Such a Community of faith—such a covenanted Community—is the world's only live demonstration of the peace-bringing Lord, who alone is the hope for peace at individual, community, national, and global levels.

They come from everywhere, with all their differences—in their ones and twos, in their tens and twenties, in their hundreds and thousands—all having this in common: They were lost and are now found, they were isolated and are now united, they were paupers and are now rich, once foolish but now wise, once rejects but now heirs. All this they are in him who is God's "yes" to all his promises and all our crying needs.[4] And we're this—not as independent units—but as part of a single Community!

Let's not have any quarreling between you and me . . .

for we are brothers.

—Genesis 13:8

✦

To Eat or Not to Eat?

However difficult it is to work out the truth Paul teaches in Romans 14:1–15:13, we're to allow it to have its way with us. It's one of those admirable sections of Scripture we become wistful over and then proceed to debate with our own vested interests safely locked away. At least, that's the temptation.

The Roman church was made up of Jews and Gentiles,[1] and because its members came from such diverse backgrounds, serious adjustments would be needed if they were to live together as the Community of the Reconciled.

A controversy arose in the church about holy days—should they be kept or not?—and about food and drink—what is kosher[2] and what's not?

THERE IS COMMUNITY

The people glaring at each other had been called by the same God, baptized into the same Christ and his elect Body, justified freely by the same grace, and called to exhibit God's redemptive and healing work to the world. So this was an "in-house" dispute.

The non-meat eaters said that eating nonkosher meats was sinful and should be stopped. They weren't saying it damned the eater;[3] had they been saying it was essential to life with God, Paul would not have tolerated the view—as he refused to tolerate the "circumcision is essential to life with God" position.[4]

But the situation was ugly enough and could have deteriorated into outright schism in the Body as a result of flared tempers, unbridled speech, and stubborn hearts. These are the usual kinds of things that hijack a genuine but nonjugular dispute and turn it into a life-and-death debate.

Paul plainly sides with the meat eaters, saying that it is no sin to eat meat. He will enter two caveats later, but he decisively says that fear of meats results from a weak grasp of truth about reality and the freedom the Messiah brings.[5]

Paul qualifies his meat-eating approval by insisting that no one should choose to do what they think is displeasing to God. To choose what you think is sinful on someone else's say-so is self-destructive, because we can't act with integrity beyond our own perceptions.[6]

But the question remained: How should they view one another?

Well, they could reflect on what God was willing to do to reconcile both sides to himself and to one another—despite their universal sinfulness.[7]

They could accept each other as servants of Christ who had given themselves to Christ on his terms.[8]

They could credit one another with intending to please God. They could look at one another and ask themselves, "Why does he eat?" or "Why does he not eat?" and give this answer: "Because he thinks it pleases God." Paul extends this credit when he says, "For none of us lives to himself alone and none of us dies to himself alone."[9] He isn't talking about our influence on each other; he's describing them as people who've given themselves to God and so eat (or don't eat) in order to please him (note v. 6).

So meat eaters could fight their irritation with their narrow and overly sensitive noneating fellow Christians and give them full credit for what they meant to do. They could rejoice at their own fuller freedom in Christ without denigrating or patronizing the not fully freed sister or brother.

Noneaters could look at the eaters and say, "Well, I think this is wrong, but they do it because they believe our Master has liberated them. I think their arguments are poor, but at least, they appeal to the one we know is Lord. And, besides, think of their background. It's a miracle that they care to please the Lord at all."

Beyond this, *they could both behave toward each other with grace,* being kind one to another, rejoicing together in areas of agreement, praising and serving the one Lord they both esteem beyond words. This would defuse the situation; it would lower the temperature. It's always easier to "hear" people we have warmth and affection for, and it's always harder to be belligerent toward those who treat us with respect and gentleness—even if we don't agree with them.

The eater could even choose to give up his right to eat. He could look at his gentle sister and brother, with their fear and bonds, and say, "Well, I don't have to eat meat. That's not the ultimate liberty Christ brought us.[10] If I can't forfeit a good steak under certain circumstances, what kind of brother am I? If I can't say no to a piece of meat, I'm the one who's bound and blind. The Christ gave up everything for them, and I'm complaining about my right to eat meat?"[11]

The eater could be warm and friendly. For Christ, fellowship, and unity's sake, he could say with Paul, "If what I eat causes [you] to fall into sin, I will never eat meat again."[12] If he did this, his abstinence would be chosen by him, not extorted from him. And of course, he'd be careful in giving this gift of abstinence to his brother and sister so that it wouldn't appear patronizing.

◆

"If I can't say no to a piece of meat, I'm the one who's bound and blind."

And what might happen during the course of continuing friendship and dialogue? Might not the noneater come to see the truth on this matter and love the abstaining brother or sister all the more for patience and service?

This is community in the Spirit, "for the kingdom of God is not a matter of eating and drinking, but of righteousness, peace and joy in the Holy Spirit."[13]

God . . . devises ways so that a banished person may not remain estranged from him.

—2 Samuel 14:14

✦

Love Will Find a Way

David's handsome son Absalom killed his half-brother and fled to Geshur where he lived for three years to avoid David's wrath. David adores Absalom and deep inside wants him back but won't make the move to restore him. His general Joab (who has his own agenda) sends a wise woman to David to see if she can get the king to bring the banished boy home. David was a sucker for a "good story," and that's what she uses to hook and reel him in (as Nathan did). In the course of her appeal, she says, "God devises ways for the estranged to get back."[1] If she had known the full Story—the blessed Story we've heard—she could really have made a case, couldn't she?

THERE IS COMMUNITY

I don't know if it's too much to say that division and fragmentation are the central fruit of human rebellion against God, but surely they must rank high. What divides people and sets them against one another is wicked. In Galatians, Paul lists the "works of the flesh," and just look how many in his list are connected with fragmentation.

Our reasons for standing apart range wide and include personal taste, disappointment in the other, bitter resentment at some real or imagined wrong, envy, insensitivity, and the like. The same things that divide families divide churches, communities, and nations.

To say that love is the cure for all this sounds trite—and yet, love *is* the cure for all this. My suspicion is—and this is hardly profound—that where there's love, it'll find a way to close gaps, tear down walls, build bridges, and create peace.

In the movie *Mr. Holland's Opus,* Mr. Holland was driven by his love of music, so he shared his passion with everyone, even those who had no musical talent. Well, not quite everyone. His son, Cole, was stone deaf, so Holland didn't bother trying to share music with him.

◆

To say that love is the cure for all this sounds trite—and yet, love is the cure for all this.

He was a good man, but his sense of loss became a quiet resentment against the deaf son, so a gulf widened between the quietly resentful father and the lonely, isolated boy—they "had nothing in common."

Then John Lennon is shot! Holland is anguished at the tragedy, and as he arrives home, his now-grown son is working on his car engine. Seeing his father's pain, the boy signs the question: "What's wrong with you?" Anguished and short of patience, the father begins to tell him about Lennon but gives up on it, saying something equivalent to, "What's the point? How could you possibly understand my pain? Lennon was a great musician and . . . ah, forget it, you wouldn't understand."

Cole is stung into anger. Does the father think he's stupid? Does he think the son doesn't know of Lennon or recognize tragedy when he meets it? Is the father the only one who has a heart and cares? How can he be so close to Lennon and care so little for his own son? And why had he shut him out of his life and music? Why hadn't he made the effort with him that he'd made with so many others? Strangers! He made the effort with strangers, for pity's sake!

His fierce anger and unanswerable points take Holland by surprise and convict him of his wrong. How could he have behaved so lovelessly? Later, when he sees Cole holding his screwdriver between his ear and the car engine to "hear" how it sounds, he's filled with remorse and works out a scheme to gain his son back and let him "hear" the music that had never been shared with him.

An evening of music is arranged, and the son is thrilled with the lights and the felt rhythm. In the middle of the proceedings, Holland announces that he wants to sing a song and dedicate it to his son. Signing as he sings, he offers a lovely piece written by John Lennon for Lennon's own child, "Beautiful Boy."[2]

> Close your eyes,
> Have no fear.
> The monster's gone;
> He's on the run,
> And your daddy's here.
> Beautiful, beautiful, beautiful,
> Beautiful boy . . .

It's a poignant and public apology—a loving father apologizing to the son he had mistreated for so long. Holland's apology proclaimed not only the human worth of the young man but the father's love for him. Love wanted and found a way, and reconciliation was the result.

Fathers and sons should be together; families should be together; friends should be together; churches, communities, and nations should be together. Humans should all be together, were all meant to be together, and that's what Jesus Christ through the Spirit works to accomplish.

How wonderful it will be when the blessed Spirit so transforms us that our individual agendas will seem less and less attractive to us. Our love for one another will deepen and become wiser, and we'll be able to work out ways to heal the wounds that keep us apart. Lovers will find a way.

People who were oppressed or in debt or dissatisfied

went to him . . . and he became their leader.

—1 Samuel 22:2 TEV

✦

ℐunday Morning

Who are these that gather themselves together on Sunday? Old and young, slow and quick, smiling and frowning, glad and sad, sick and well, alone and with families. Who are they? In their Sunday-go-to-meeting clothes or in their casuals, from out of town and just around the corner, the eager and the bored, the cynical and the expectant, on time and running late.

And what do the neighbors think as they peek out from behind their curtains, pass them in the street, or nod at them from the doorstep? What do they think as they hear the hymns dancing or marching or struggling through the air? What do they think when they "hear" the silences between the hymns and know that this is the time when prayers of confession, petition, thanksgiving, adoration, and lament are being raised to God?

And why do they come? God knows! At different times they come with different moods and for different reasons. To see friends, because parents make them go, because it's expected of them, because their children need them to, because a pretty girl or a handsome boy will be there, because . . .

I suppose we've all shared in the bad, poor, or doubtful reasons for congregating, but there are times when, by God's grace, we get it right, and we gather for the very best reasons.

We're never so visibly one as when we make an appointment at a given place and a given time for a given purpose—and keep it.

Sometimes we come together simply to thank God. And we have so much to be thankful for! Clean water, warm beds, fresh coffee, delicious food, parks, rivers, decent clothes, children to love and be loved by, parents who care, friends to run to for help, friends who need our help, jobs to go to, forgiveness given and received, warm sunshine, cool rain, doctors and hospitals, grandchildren to climb all over us, grabbing at our spectacles or sucking on our knuckles, Christ who died for us, the Spirit who nurtures us. All of this! And so we come just to tell him "thanks."

✦

We're never so visibly one as when we make an appointment at a given place and a given time for a given purpose—and keep it.

Sometimes we come to find forgiveness. We know the church doesn't forgive us; we know forgiveness doesn't come from the preacher; we know it isn't found in the place or even the service of worship. We know all that, but sometimes it's there—there where the living Christ honors us by being present at holy Communion, there with our sisters and brothers where faith is deepened and commitment is renewed, there where humble confession seems especially appropriate—there we come to find forgiveness. And we leave feeling cleansed!

Sometimes we come to find challenge and encouragement. We don't want our sins whitewashed, don't want them minimized; we get enough of that in the work-a-day world. And we don't want—at least we don't want to want—to simply drift along lifeless. We'd like to be stirred out of our banal life; we'd like to be filled with the wind of the Spirit, to be carried to places we'd never choose to go, making decisions we never thought we'd make. We'd like to make our mark for Christ. Without ballyhoo or trumpets blowing, without hoopla or red carpets, we'd like to live strong, clean, and with a joy-filled stubbornness that makes the world take notice of the Spirit in our lives.

Sometimes we come simply to worship and adore. The immensity of life sometimes overwhelms us—reality is just too huge for us to take in, much less control. "A little speck of a planet orbiting a smaller-than-average star in a backwater galaxy"—that's how some astronomers describe our home. You'd have to have a search warrant and an angelic host of seekers to find us, if you didn't have special guidance.

But it's more than the size; it's the mystery of it all—the unanswered questions, the questions we can't quite frame, the questions we're half afraid to be able to frame. If he's half the God we read, pray, and sing he is, why would he bother with this sludge-filled, galactic bayou?

The God who rolled out space like someone laying carpet, who measured the oceans in his cupped hands, and who scattered giant suns like a jeweler's diamonds on the black velvet of the night—

you don't shake hands with a God like that and be content to call him "chum."

And the God who is so holy that he took the sin of this little backwater planet so seriously that the whole universe was out of harmony until he dealt with it—that God sometimes fills us with awe, occasionally dread.

And so sometimes we come to hear the Story of God's search for us. If it weren't for that Story, the size, the mystery, and the holiness would keep us from coming at all. It's there we learn that we're "the visited planet" and that the holy Lord would not let us roll in our sin and misery but came to rescue us and fill the universe with joy and richness. Driving the wrong kind of darkness from every corner of this vast universe, he makes our planet a home rather than a whirling Alcatraz.

And so we file into our usual seats, nod in the usual directions, smiling and sometimes fussing to get the kids settled. Then together with the saints, we become a Community of witness for the living Lord.

All that we do, we do together as a body of people. Together we sing as the people of God! As a congregation of his people, we pray even when one person shapes the prayer for us. As an assembly of his people, we place ourselves under the judgment, consolation, enlightenment, rebuke, and assurance of the Word of God as it comes to us through a member of our Community. In previous days, we spent some of the money God blessed us with to pay honorable debts and make honorable provision for our families—all to God's pleasure. Now as one body, we give money to feed the poor, carry the Message, and assist the assembly to carry out its purposes.

Some days we're blessed to see a trusting and repentant person baptized into union with Christ, and we see the gospel enacted before our gathered eyes.

And as his covenanted Community and because it pleases him, we set apart bread and wine in a covenant renewal. It is here that we meet the living Christ, who communes with us by his Holy Spirit who dwells among us. And while the sanctified bread and wine remains bread and wine, it is no longer merely bread and wine. When we spread the Table, this sovereign Lord of ours graciously makes himself present. The bread and wine become more than symbols of his body and blood; they become signs of his holy presence. And our holy communion becomes holy Communion, so we can whisper as we eat the bread, "He's here!" And in our eating, we become "proclaimers" of his death, life, and his glorious return.[1]

And not alone do we do this! We gather together as his people, and as his people we eat the Supper with our Lord.

That's community. That's why we "go to church." We're needy, dissatisfied, oppressed, overwhelmed with life, lonely, sinful, floating, and longing for better. In that condition, we went out to Christ and do continue to go out to him to make him our Leader.

Aim at integrity, faith, love and peace, in the company of
those who invoke the Lord out of a pure heart.
—2 Timothy 2:22 MOFFATT

✦

Some Anti-Class Remarks

What follows needs to be balanced and refined, but in the middle of it all, I think there's something useful we need to take seriously. Perhaps you could discuss the material with your friends, discover and develop the useful, and jettison the useless.

Concerning the education of the Church, I'm in favor of having different classes for different groups, especially the very young. But there are real dangers in our "fragmenting" every time we get together—even if we do it with the best intentions.

There's the danger of creating little churches within the congregation, the danger of stressing our differences too much and not what's common to us. Classes can become "group therapy" sessions and the Bible little more than a book we search through for answers to "my" problems. This approach distorts the nature of the Scriptures and sees them as a psychology manual or a source of answers in a "dilemma ethics" course. Is our purpose for coming together to get therapy and advice about specific dilemmas? Is this what "Bible study" is about? Is this what "worship" is about?[1]

Well, "We need different classes because we have different needs," someone responds. And so, should our assemblies become "need driven"? Should our needs determine what we discuss and how we approach Scripture?[2]

A reasonable response is, "But we all really do have different needs." Well, we do and we don't. My suspicion is that our needs are all pretty much alike. Peer pressure; fear of what the future holds; loneliness; a quest for purity, honesty, and integrity; the need for a healthy self-respect; financial struggles; parent/child difficulties; wrestling with guilt and shame, with disablement and chronic illness—not one of these is related to any particular age, gender, or social group.

One young man reminded me that teenagers have sexual drives to wrestle with. I asked him if he thought older men and women like me had up and died. He spoke of peer pressure and the drive for success, and I assured him that in some ways these can be tougher for the older set. That's how it went. Our discussion ended with each of us thinking we had a good case. Which is no doubt true!

I know that our common challenges and pains have different ways of showing themselves in the young and the old, but I'm insisting that our problems boil down to common denominators. We're all in the same arena, battling the same foes and facing the same challenges! We're not all equally experienced and capable, which is why we need to be running interference for one another.

And I know that the young can offer insights to their peers

about how to face certain situations they have in common. But even here, we assume they all face specifically similar situations because they're all young. I think this is no more true than it is to say all older people face the very same things because they're older.

Situations are shaped, colored, and made different by the person who faces them. No two people face precisely the same situation. So rather than endlessly working with "dilemma ethics" (What should I do if . . . ?), we need to spend much of our time shaping the person. What we most often need when facing "dilemmas" isn't *knowledge* but the *character* to live out what we already know.[3]

♦

Rather than endlessly working with "dilemma ethics," we need to spend much of our time shaping the person.

The claim is made that couples don't have time for "single people"; thus, the singles need a class of their own. So the solution for a bad case of isolation is to create more? In doing so, the couples aren't confronted over their fragmenting behavior, and the understandable disappointment of the singles is allowed to fester—and the two groups go their separate ways.

The older people and the teens have nothing in common, we're told. Is the solution, then, to encourage teens to keep to themselves in the "general assembly" in addition to their already separate class? This is healthy?

But I thought our message was that we have in common all that is of eternal consequence. What would happen if teenagers "invaded" the classes of the older folks on a regular basis, sat by them, shared a Bible and hymnal, bowed their heads together, and had the occasional giggle? Is there anything finer than seeing a family unit sing, pray, and commune together?

Given the fact that we only meet briefly in our assemblies, is it wise to structure fragmentation? I don't think that laying down anti-class laws is the answer—even if we agreed there was a problem here—but in the light of who the Church of God is and is to be (the Community of the Reconciled), in light of our tendency to isolate each other, in light of the hunger "to belong" even while we fragment so easily, perhaps it wouldn't hurt to review the whole matter, to ask for input, and to try some things that would promote joyous, assembly-wide fellowship.

Over the long haul, our assemblies, however we structure them, need to remind us that we are a Community and not merely a crowd of people who use the same building for separate groups that focus on distinctive needs. It's that aspect of this subject that I think we need to examine with great care. It can't be wise for us always to be stressing the things that separate us rather than those that make us one and bring us together.[4]

When I smiled at them, they scarcely believed it;
the light of my face was precious to them.
—Job 29:24

✦

The Outer Fringe

God knows our sinfulness, but he also knows our inner longings. He sees our failures, but he takes note of the genuineness of
our aims. He sees beyond our wicked deeds. Behind and under
our sinful attitudes, he sees our hunger for faithfulness. And we
know he doesn't despise us; we know he doesn't think we're an
endless burden he has to "put up with."

We tremble in his presence because we lack the deeper holiness
we seek, but we don't have to compete with him—he's out of our
league. We don't have to persuade him to be gracious toward us,
for we know he is and always has been. We ask his forgiveness and
feel assured that it's freely given. So it isn't what *he* thinks about us

that often makes us feel despondent; it's what *you* think—you, the upright, the fast horses in the church stable.

God help us, we're so pathetic that if you won't smile at us, won't give us plenty of assurance that we're worth having in the family—if you won't do that—we shrivel and nearly die of loneliness.

We tell ourselves it shouldn't matter, that God's view of us is all that counts, that after all, it was Christ who died and lives for us. We should be able to live without your warm approval, but we can't. Our human need for human warmth won't let us live without you.

We should be able to live without your warm approval, but we can't.

We know about Paul's "there's neither Jew nor Greek, bond or free, male or female" in Christ. We don't doubt the truth of this scripture, but it's the categories "weak" and "strong" that get our attention. We don't think we're being pushed or chilled out; we're not deliberately ignored or passed by; we're not unwanted or despised—we just feel like it sometimes. In the end, the problem isn't really with you, it's with us, but we don't seem to be able to do anything about it, so we depend on you to go that extra mile.

And it all sounds so wimpy when we say it, even to ourselves. If you pressed us with, "And what exactly do you want?" we probably couldn't put it into words, and that makes it worse. If we couldn't tell you, we think you'd shrug and walk off leaving us feeling even more idiotic. We'd go off home and snarl at ourselves in the mirror, "Well, what *do* you want?"

It's not that we're wrestling with great sins in our lives—though many of us are and wouldn't dream of telling you—it's just that we feel we're not good enough, not involved enough, not something enough to be secure about our place in the fellowship. We feel like an appendix—we're part of the body, but nobody knows what we're good for. Your words of tolerant acceptance are just that: tolerance, not equality. There's no way we'd think you "need" us. We wouldn't be the ones you'd introduce to your non-Christian friends as you "cultivated" them for Christ. At best, we're warm bodies that swell the crowd at assembly periods.

And listen, we don't need you to be our close friends—no one can be a close friend to everyone—but we need you to smile at us, warm and genuine, need you to make it easy for us to be in your presence. We don't need you to have us over to eat all the time. We can't visit around that many houses, life is too demanding for that. Just give us the impression that you would *want* to have us, that you think being in our company for a few hours would not only be pleasant but somehow enriching, as if we had something to offer you.

We need to feel like contributors to the body rather than tolerated appendages. Help us believe what we have trouble believing: that we're secure and well thought of in Christ and that that's how Christ has led you to think of us.

Do what you can to create an air of acceptance in the assembly. There's so much demanded of believers, yet sometimes all we can do is tread water—barely surviving. Do what you can to convince us that you joyfully receive what Paul calls the "less honorable" and even "unpresentable" parts of the body.[1]

You might think there's only a few of us, but this isn't true. We're in every assembly, and we number in the thousands. And we're a pain in the neck. We'll irritate you, and—if you don't have plenty of helpers as you work with us—we'll wear you out. But do your very best to remember that you're the Spirit's gift to us and that you yourself live by his sustaining grace.[2]

And when his work in and through you has its desired effect, we'll bless your name, giving God thanks for you. We'll become to others what you've been and are to us—people who embody the unity of the Spirit and who nurture joyful peace among disciples whose personal stories differ so widely.

For our part, we'll do our best to live a life worthy of our calling, to expect great things from God, to honor and love his people, and not to whine. By the grace of the Spirit, if we can't give you a lot of positive input, we'll try hard not to make your every visit with us a draining experience. We'd hate it, too, if every time you saw us coming, you prepared yourself for another unloading session.

We do rejoice; help our lack of joy. We do feel wanted; help our sense of unwantedness. We do feel secure; help us in our insecurity. Make us feel fully welcomed into your presence, even as we're fully welcomed into the presence of the Father.

Who is weak, and I do not feel his weakness?
—2 Corinthians 11:29 MOFFATT

✦

On Our Side of the Gulf

If someone were to claim that his virtue and graces were developed without anyone's help, we'd think he was crazy or arrogant or a little of both. We all helped to generate and nurture the virtues he prizes so highly. Grandparents, parents, Sunday-school and grade-school teachers, ministers, writers, friends—a host of people he knows and a greater host he doesn't. He is not and cannot be virtuous alone! He's part of a Community, whether he realizes it or not.

We're a Community of fellow sufferers, and when one hurts, we all feel the hurt—or at least, in our better moments we want to. We don't want these people to stand alone, isolated, and we'd think it a shame if they had to. We're a Community of blessed people, too, and we aren't so envious that we can't rejoice in the good fortune of our friends, brothers, and sisters. Granted that that's more difficult for some of us than others, and it's even more difficult if we're going through a bad spell. Still, we can and do rise to finding pleasure in their joy.

We're also a Community of fellow sinners, but sharing and bearing the blame with sinners is a horse of a different color.

I won't waste your time stressing the obvious—that we're personally responsible for our sin and that we must see that or be made to see it; it must be brought home to us and dealt with as peculiarly ours. This must be done for all kinds of good reasons. Okay, I've said what no sane person with a Bible in their hand would dream of doubting.

But what I want to stress is this: No one sins alone! My sin is *peculiarly* mine, but it is not exclusively mine. I know passages that convict certain sinners of their sin, and I've no wish to deny them. I'm only interested in stressing another truth, a truth that so many upright people choke on: No one sins alone! No one is exclusively responsible for his sin. This is a hard saying, but I know it's true.

◆

My sin is peculiarly mine, but it is not exclusively mine.

Ezra came from Babylon to work with the community and found it in a moral and religious shambles. His response was this: "O my God, I am ashamed, I blush to lift my face to thee, my God, for our iniquities are higher than our heads, our guilt has reached the skies."[1]

This is more than compassion for sinners; it's identification with them in their crimes. But how could he share the blame? Why is he blushing and feeling shame? Why does he speak of "our" sins? Well, perhaps he was just being "nice" and counted himself in, though he didn't mean to be taken too seriously. Does a reading of the text suggest anything like that? There's nothing even *remotely* like that in the text.

It would have been right to say, "O God, we come on behalf of those who've sinned and ask that you will indeed forgive them!" It would be right, I tell you! It would also be right to say, "Dear Lord, have mercy on our brothers and sisters. We know they've sinned, but life is hard, and we all struggle with one thing or another."

But that's not what Ezra said! It just isn't good enough to say about sinners, "Their sin isn't mine!" Ezra (and Daniel[2]) said, "Their sin is ours!"

For good or ill, we help to shape one another. We're a world of sinners, nations of sinners, cities, towns, villages, and communities of sinners. We're families and congregations of sinners, and to speak or act as though we haven't contributed to each other's wickedness is simply nonsense. No one governs a nation, writes a book, drives a cab, mothers a child, is husband to a wife, serves at a checkout, or does anything alone, because we're social beings.

And when we sin, we infect the air! Our refusal to admit wrongs provokes bitterness, our coldness makes others frosty, and our brutality makes people vicious. Our needless severity generates isolation and shuts people up in their sin. Our smugness curls lips, our greed begets Scrooges, and our bullying creates cowards. We tirelessly criticize and our children pass it on to their children, and they to theirs, in ever-widening circles. We withhold praise, and thousands wither and die.

We generalize, and hosts resent it; we won't keep our word, and distrust flourishes; we're suspicious, and the world's more cynical. We speak and write infectious sewage, and people are degraded; we're merciless, and harshness is born in others; we're vengeful, and others begin to keep records. We insinuate, withhold, imply, suggest, and hint, and the air is filled with rumor, fears, and insecurities.

Barriers go up, gaps appear, bridges fall into disrepair, homes go unvisited, budding friendships die from neglect, communication becomes desultory, a nod and a thin smile replace warmth and laughter, pain at bad news is replaced with a shrug of the shoulders, and life is less life. We glare at a checkout girl or "prefer not to get involved" or can't be bothered to put ourselves out, and a network of evil is spawned or strengthened. Aside from a handful of "bleeding heart liberals" (who don't always make sense!), we have an awful time accepting the truth of all this.

I've sat by myself, grinding my teeth over my sin, *and at the same time,* believing it wasn't *all* my fault. Not daring to ask others to share the blame, not daring to ask others to admit that we're all implicated in my sin.

I know this is a hard saying, for I've been on the receiving end of injustice and pressed the crime home to the transgressor. I didn't want him to tell me how others contributed to his sin; I wanted him to feel the searing shame. I didn't want him to share responsibility with anyone—least of all with me, whom he'd cruelly used.

But it doesn't matter how I felt—the truth is the truth! It's still true that we should see sin as more pervasive, less atomized, less strictly "yours" or "mine," "his" or "hers"—and more "ours." I'm suggesting that the sin of one of us is in some real sense the sin of all of us.

In our saner moments, we wouldn't dream of saying that only a handful of first-century people crucified the Christ. To thousands of strangers from distant lands, Peter said, "You, with the help of wicked men, put him to death by nailing him to the

cross."[3] However we work it all out, we know they were all implicated in the crucifixion of the Master—just as we are.

It's breathtaking that we should even imagine that we walk
through life—that we have ever walked through life—spreading
only holiness in all its beauty. We'd have to have a very high opin-
ion of ourselves or a shallow view of sin to think the only thing
we've contributed to all the lives we've touched down the years is
generosity, redemptive holiness, humility, and a glad willingness
to forgive. Who are we kidding?

But beyond all that, do you know what's really staggering? It's
the way Christ responded to the sin of his nation and of the
world. Christ, who really did go through life spreading nothing
but purity and encouragement, identified himself with sinners—
didn't distance himself from them at all. He was personally sinless,
but he stood in line as one of a sinful nation to be baptized with
a baptism of repentance! Can you believe it? Are you willing to
embrace it? is a more searching question. Here's how one man put
this almost incredible truth about Christ:

> The sinless Sufferer on the cross, in His oneness with His
> brethren, felt their wrong-doing His own, confessed in
> His forsakenness that God would have nothing to do
> with it except destroy it, felt that it separated between
> men and God, and that he was actually away from God
> . . . that He with his recoil and quiver should still have
> loved us so intensely that, when He felt the gulf fixed
> between God and sinners, He thought Himself on our
> side of the breach and numbered Himself with the trans-
> gressors—that is the marvel.[4]

As sickening as sin was to him, as dear as his Father was to him,
Jesus joined us on our side of the gulf that was between God and

man. And we go to great lengths to distance ourselves from sinners? Claiming this is the way of the Christ?

I know in my bones that what Henry Sloane Coffin said is true: "Only sin-bearing and sin-sharing people can truly represent the Savior of sinners!"[5]

There is none righteous, no not one, and when they sin, we're all indicted! Tell us the truths that balance that truth some other time. For now, encourage us to see and embrace this truth before us. Allow us to reflect on the Christ who stands with sinners on our side of the gulf. It ought to remind us that smugness is out of place in sinners. It should remind us that Jesus takes seriously the matter of stone-throwing. For the thrower has forgotten that in another setting, he would be the one in the middle of the ring with stones falling on him.

CHAPTER SIX

Where the Spirit of the Lord Is...

THERE IS TRUTH

The word of God is not for sale; and
therefore it has no need of shrewd salesmen.
The word of God is not seeking patrons;
therefore it refuses price cutting and bargaining.
. . . It does not care to be sold at any price.
It only desires to be its own genuine self.

—Karl Barth

♦

Truth and the Believer

Christians aren't supposed to worship the Bible—that'd be idolatry. They aren't supposed to erect a shrine to the great god "Truth," because behind all truth, biblical or otherwise, is an inexpressibly lovely Person who reveals himself so we can have a relationship with him.

Imagine this: While I'm away on a trip, my wife writes me this lovely letter, telling me how she feels about me and what she wants for both of us. She picks me up at the airport on my return; I peck her on the cheek and begin to read the letter. We make the long drive in silence as I read and glow. I give brief answers to some of her questions as I read the letter, and that night I set the alarm for every other hour, so I can wake and read the letter. She has spent the day ignored and now lies by my side alone and silent.

You think she's pleased with my devotion to the letter? Wouldn't she say something like, "Would you rip that thing up and talk to me!"? I might protest that I just love her letter and want to absorb it. She would tell me she didn't write the letter to have it get between us. She wrote it, revealing her heart, so we would be drawn closer together!

So it is with biblical truths. They're not written to be analyzed, admired, proclaimed, rehearsed, and memorized. (Yes, they are!) They're more than ethical instructions; they're more than the revelation of humans as they are and could be; they're more than poetry, history, legal materials, promise, and protest. In the hands of the Spirit, they're the life-creating Story of a holy and sovereign God and his continuing, loving pursuit of rebellious humans. They're the assurance that this whole creation is being carried along by that holy Lord to a grand and glorious conclusion.

They're a treasure committed by God into the believers' hearts and hands so that the believers can be shaped and sustained in this world while they function as a Community of Witness.

We revere the Scriptures, but they're no substitute for our Lord and Master. We will not allow them to vanish from the world, but neither will we allow them to displace God as the center of our lives.

Having said that, we do revere and trust the Bible! It's our protection against those who pour out oracles saying they heard them from God in secret. Down the ages, believers have relied on the Scriptures to test the spirits to see if they're of God. When foundational questions are asked, they've followed their Master and wanted to know, "What do the Scriptures say?"[1] And while there hasn't always been agreement on what the Bible teaches, there's been agreement that what didn't have the support of Scripture was suspect at best and false at worst.

And that matters! For in the end, it's truth we want, truth we must have. In a world of lies and wild guesses, a world of maybes and relativism, a world that skirts tough questions and prefers sentiment, God pity us, we need truth!

When he, the Spirit of truth, comes,

he will guide you into all truth.

—John 16:13

◆

Camels and Gnats

All truth is truth, but some of it doesn't shake the world. It's true that I once failed my parallel-parking test during my driving exam. But who cares? And why should anyone? I don't even care!

Jesus Christ is Lord! Now there's a truth that reverberates throughout the universe. And that's the central truth the Holy Spirit carries throughout the world: The crucified Jesus died an atoning death in a self-surrender that sprang out of holy love; God raised him from the dead and has made him Lord![1]

The One made Lord is God's Prince and Champion on behalf of the human race, against all the forces of darkness, which have betrayed, demented, and damned it. He came and, by the Spirit of God, cast out demons, binding the "strong man," setting free his prisoners, and serving notice to all the powers—in and out of this world—that he was on a mission of rescue and would not be turned from it.[2]

Maybe the gospel story is all nonsense; maybe he never came at all. But this much we know: *If* he came, he came to do harm only to that and to those who make themselves enemies of God and the world he loves so much. Say the story is all false; say Freud was right, that it's all wishing. But let us at least understand its claim: In Jesus Christ, God has come looking for us—and not to harm us, no, never to harm us!

Now, if this is true—and it is—surely this is the truth we ought to be proclaiming. This is the truth that can change a universe or a world or a single life. Other things must be discussed and taught, of course! But certainly, compared with this, so much truth is downright trivia.[3]

♦

Compared with the truth that Jesus is Lord, so much truth is downright trivia.

Assure a child that some milk comes from a cow, and you've told him a truth, you've given him information, you've freed him from ignorance. But assure him that his father, who is off working in some distant land, still loves him deeply, and you've stabilized and brightened his whole world. There's information and *information*; there's freedom and *freedom*.

When Zerubbabel and his company left for Judea, they took with them 435 camels.[4] That's truth, but it isn't the kind of truth that men and women gladly live by or die for. On the day they left, if there had been only 430 camels, Nehemiah would have told that truth, but we can't and shouldn't believe that God expects us to rejoice in Nehemiah 7:69 as we rejoice in, say, John 10:1–18.

Truths in Scripture (as in life) don't function the way words in a crossword puzzle do—if you get one word wrong, the whole

204

thing is incomplete. In crossword puzzles, every word is equally important, but that's not how the Bible is structured. No, multiplied millions have lived and died rejoicing in God and the indispensable truths the Spirit has brought while remaining ignorant of so much of the biblical Story.

The truths of Scripture are all interrelated; they have no independent significance. They are part of the single movement of the Creator Spirit toward his creation, as he works through individuals and nations to bring the Story to a glorious conclusion. The Christ insisted that some matters in the Spirit's "Law and Prophets" are "more important" than others,[5] and he also spoke of "the least" of the commandments.[6]

There is no suggestion in these words that any truth is unimportant—the reverse is true. All truth is important, even the truth conveyed by the "least stroke of a pen"[7]; and those who love the One who called himself "the Truth"[8] honor it wherever they find it. Every truth, without exception, is part of the overall Message, and it isn't for us to rewrite the Spirit's work, dispensing with truths as we go.

To be led by the Spirit to confess Jesus as Lord is to be brought into truth that has consequences for our eternal destiny, our character, vision, chosen behaviors, attitudes, and decision-making criteria. And the final outcome of all this is *freedom* in the richest sense of the word.[9]

A response to all this, as I see it, should be that we rejoice in every truth, despising none, honoring all, but majoring in majors, "keeping the main thing the main thing." Even though that's a tall order, it's not an impossible order! It's one we're obliged to undertake and one that's worth all the trouble it takes.

To speak of every truth as equally important may rise out of a pious spirit, but it isn't wise. It would lead sensitive believers to spend much of their limited time in areas hardly related to the needs of their lives and their place in this world. They would struggle to understand and remember every piece of biblical information from Genesis 1 to Revelation 22 and hold each piece with passionate conviction. They would neglect truths that are of immediate and vital importance to their faith in and their commitment to Jesus their Lord.

Is this not precisely what the Master was speaking about when he spoke of "more important matters" and binding "heavy loads"?[10]

The good news is, while many of us claim, for one theological reason or another, that all truths are equally important, we practice no such thing. We don't give equal time and energy to the study and teaching (much less to the practice) of vast areas of Scripture. We stress, year in, year out, what appear to be the most fruitful sections of Scripture without despising any other.

The bad news is, while many of us claim that all truths are equally important, we incessantly harp on the same truths to the same people, saying the same things for the same reasons decade after decade.

I suspect that one of the ways we can show that all truths are important, even if they aren't the "more important matters," is by the way we handle the Bible as a whole. As best we can determine with the Spirit's help, we're to give every section its God-given place in the unfolding Story.

There are biblical truths that cause less than a ripple in our lives. There are others that subvert our view of ourselves and the world we live in and have eternal consequences—affecting our whole salvation, our inner shaping, our life in and view of the world. And all of this, because they bring before us truths like *Jesus is Lord!*

Open my eyes that I may see
wonderful things in your law.
—Psalm 119:18

✦

Holy Spirit or Blueprint?

It's wrong to set the Holy Spirit over against what he has clearly revealed, placing his word in opposition to himself. This just won't do! We can't despise the clear word of the Spirit and pretend we're honoring him.

So when we reflect on "Holy Spirit or Blueprint?" I've no wish to set the Spirit against his biblical word. It isn't an either-or matter!

But we must allow the Spirit to be sovereign. We must allow him to determine the nature of his biblical revelation. I'm opposed to the notion that the Holy Spirit presents us with an exhaustive blueprint when he gives us the Bible. And, like thousands of others before me, I'm opposed to the notion that he gave us a "complete guide to living" and then vanished, leaving us without help and to our own devices.

To say the Spirit guided the church into "all truth" through the apostolic and prophetic witness is to agree with a plain utterance of Scripture, but to say that that means he delivered us an exhaustive blueprint is false. To say that God has given us all we need related to life and godliness[1] is to repeat Scripture, but to say that that means he left no questions that need working out is clearly untrue. There are a host of questions he helps us answer without exhaustive instructions! This should come as no surprise to anyone. You can't open the Bible without being confronted with unanswered ethical questions. Let me illustrate:

What verses give explicit answers to questions like these: Is genetic engineering morally acceptable? What about harvesting human organs from "spare embryos"? Is playing the lottery a good thing? How much should I give to support church programs? Is it okay to have shares in a company that uses slave labor to make its products? Is cloning humans immoral? Is the death penalty a Christian choice? Should Christians bomb innocent civilians in war? Should Christians engage in war at all?

Has the Spirit told us exhaustively and precisely how we are to respond to the following ethical teachings?

> Forfeit your liberties!
> Be modest in dress!
> Don't be greedy!
> Honor your parents!
> Obey the government!
> Give as you've been prospered!
> Return not evil for evil!
> Suffer yourselves to be defrauded!
> Love Christ above family!

208

I think we all know that these things are debated and puzzled over, day in and day out, by good-hearted and responsible believers. Why is that so? Because the Spirit hasn't seen fit to give out exhaustive answers and prescriptions.

If we want an exhaustive blueprint, we need more than rules—we need instructions on how the rules are to be kept, instructions the Spirit didn't see fit to write down. Here are just a few illustrations of what I mean from the Old Covenant Scriptures, which are supposed to be "legalistic" and brimful of details.

"Don't work on the Sabbath" sounds simple until you ask what *work* entails. "Leave the crops at the edges of your fields for the poor" is plain until someone asks what *edges* means and who exactly is poor. "Don't offer an animal with a blemish" is no problem if nobody asks, "What exactly constitutes a blemish?" "Love your neighbor as yourself" is central, but where are the verses that exhaustively explain what that entails in any and all circumstances? The law says "Stone the adulterous one," but what if, like Hosea or Joseph or Jesus, we don't want to?

Yes, I'm sure we all can come up with some sensible comments on all these issues and topics, but that's just it—we have to come up with them; the Spirit didn't spell them out.

What then? Is everything up for grabs? No, everything is not up for grabs, and although the Spirit has not given exhaustive and explicit instructions for every question about life, there is no need to panic. He has revealed enough. He has revealed all we need without an exhaustive blueprint.

But how will we know how to please God if he doesn't give us all the answers? Well, he *hasn't* given us all the answers, so it must be possible to

♦

God hasn't given us all the answers, so it must be possible to please him without them.

209

please God without them. The Spirit does something better than that!

Let me oversimplify, hopefully without leading anyone tragically astray. Determining the will of God involves some foundational information and a heart lovingly committed to him.

In the information area, there are some truths we can't operate without. You know the kind of thing I mean. Ephesians 4:1–6 and Romans 13:8–10 give us a glimpse of the direction we would go with that.

When the information limit is reached (that is, when there are no texts that deal explicitly with our questions) and we have decisions that must be made, we aren't supposed to think the Spirit has cheated us. We're supposed to rely on the way he has been shaping us into Christ's image.

The famous composer Franz Joseph Haydn died, leaving a number of unfinished musical scores that were recently uncovered. A lover of his work, one of the foremost experts in the field, wrote endings for some of them. He knew, as we all know, that there's no way to be sure exactly how Haydn would have finished these pieces. But we do know the kind of way he would have done it, because someone who had drunk the spirit of the composer, who honored and rejoiced in his work, who ate, slept, and drank his thought, who had poured himself into the mold and mind of the man—someone like that carried the unfinished work to a Haydn-like conclusion. He came to Haydn-like conclusions because he had become Hadyn-like in his musical heart and thought.[2]

And that's part of what the Spirit of God does to, in, and for us. We steep ourselves in his Word with hearts that seek to follow his work of glorifying Christ. We become "spiritual," beginning to have the mind of the Spirit so that in the absence of an exhaustive blueprint that says what we should do, we come up with a Christ-like, a Spiritlike conclusion.

We cannot be dead certain what Christ would do if he were faced with some of our dilemmas, but if we become like him, we'll know the kind of response he would make!

"What would Jesus do?" is a great question, but we can only ask it because we don't have his written and explicit response to our dilemmas. If we had all the answers to all the questions, there'd be no room to ask what he would want us to do—we'd just turn to the text and read it!

Should I buy into the tobacco company? Should I marry previously divorced John? Should I tell rich young men to sell all they have and give it to the poor? Should I tell the brand-new Christian to quit his job in the bar immediately? Should I cancel my HBO subscription? In a host of such matters, "What would Jesus do?" means we have to work without explicit verses. And unless our situation is precisely what his was, we have even less than an explicit text.

Like it or not, we don't have an inexhaustible supply of "Here's precisely what you should do when this or that arises." What does that tell us?

It says we mustn't need such a supply. It says we can get along very well without it since the Spirit didn't give it!

Besides, we'd need a book the size of a continent to spell out our every response to every situation for every individual.

And what's more, why would we think it healthy if life with God boiled down to spending our lives searching for prepackaged answers for every conceivable situation? Life like that would not only be impossible—it would be impoverished. Imagine your children living like that?

Information matters! But knowing the will of God goes

beyond searching the Bible for the right verse or principles that deal with our specific questions. There's something better in every way: "Let your minds be remade and your whole nature thus transformed. Then you will be able to discern the will of God, and to know what is good, acceptable, and perfect."[3]

As the Spirit of God transforms us from glory to increasing glory into the likeness of Christ,[4] we "see" better and fathom things that were formerly beyond us. We've been given all we need: the Holy Spirit, enough clearly revealed truth, and character transformation. The Spirit is creating a people of character who will glorify God, even where exhaustive instructions don't exist.

I've loved and been loved by Ethel for more than forty-two years, and I've learned, because of the intimacy of the relationship down the years, what it is that pleases or grieves her. Some of that knowledge comes from her having expressly said this or that, but so much of it comes without her having to spell it out. I'm not saying words ever become useless, even less that they are despised; but I'm saying that words are a way to an intimacy that transcends the words. Not only do I understand who and what she is through her words, I understand who and what she is through the intimacy of our relationship, and that helps me understand her words at a level strangers can't. Who does that surprise? No one.

It's no news that the best and most sensitive interpreter of a loved one's words and movement in life is the one who loves and is loved by that person. And it's hardly profound to say that the most sensitive and best interpreter of the Spirit is one who loves and is loved by the Spirit. The deeper the intimacy, the greater the understanding.

One of the results of loving intimacy is that a few words yield more truth to the lover than a library of books reveals to the stranger.

Take a single biblical illustration. Ancient Israel was told, "When you reap the harvest of your land, do not reap to the very edges of your field or gather the gleanings of your harvest. . . . Leave them for the poor and the alien."[5]

No text precisely defines "edges" ("corners" in older versions) or "the poor." This lack of precision is normal, even though it provokes "decision time." The compilers of the Mishnah even have a booklet called "Corners," which deals with gleaning and harvesting any area that the Torah left unspecified.[6]

How close to the edge is allowed? The text doesn't say. So, were they left in the dark? They were not! Some farmers might have come out with their measuring rods and slide rules, but that wouldn't have helped since no length was legislated.

Why didn't God specify? Because he didn't want to! How did he expect people to obey if he didn't specify?

At the end of the piece we're talking about (as with so many in this section), he simply said, "I am the Lord your God."[7] And that was what they were to use as a measuring stick. This "Lord" (*Yahweh*) was the one who, in lavish grace, pitied them, delivered them from captivity, blessed them abundantly, and now dwelt among them, receiving them as his people.

With that in mind, they were to look at the poor, look at their fields at harvest time, and act like God.

For those who came out with slide rules, grammars, lexicons, and various translations of the text—an exhaustive blueprint wasn't their problem.

Lovers don't need an exhaustive blueprint from the Spirit! The desire to please God and not oneself makes good interpreters.

There was a time when his peers claimed they weren't certain if the Christ was speaking the truth. The problem, they assured him, lay in his teaching. It was all a matter of "truth," don't you see? They had to have "the truth." They could hardly submit to it if it weren't "the truth," and since he had not been under the guidance of a recognized rabbi,[8] they couldn't be sure.

The Master responded: "If anyone chooses to do God's will, he will find out whether my teaching comes from God or whether I speak on my own. He who speaks on his own does so to gain honor for himself, but he who works for the honor of the one who sent him is a man of truth; there is nothing false about him. Has not Moses given you the law? Yet not one of you keeps the law."[9]

✦

The desire to please God and not oneself makes good interpreters.

They had the law of Moses, which they insisted was truth, and they were ignoring that. Christ didn't claim his teaching was his own—the reverse was true.[10] But he did claim to seek the honor of the one who sent him, and this was the assurance that what he was speaking he had heard from God. They had received the law from Moses but continued to speak on their own. They weren't listening to Moses, so why should he expect them to listen to him?[11]

"His hearers," says Leon Morris, "had raised the question of His competence as a teacher. He raises the question of their competence as hearers."[12]

The genuine desire to obey enables us to see things we would have missed and evaporates many "theological problems" with its warm breath of eager submission.

Whatever you do, whether in word or deed, do it all in the
name of the Lord Jesus, giving thanks to God the
Father through him.

—Colossians 3:17

✦

Changing Jobs?

As we go through life, there are questions we must answer for which we have no texts. If God has a specific plan for every step of our lives, he hasn't seen fit to reveal it, so we have to work with that fact.

It complicates things if we believe that the Spirit has an exhaustive plan for our lives, as if he had a graph on his wall with our lives mapped out step by step. What happens if he has x and we do y? How are we to know? What does that do to the graph on the Spirit's wall?

I know no biblical reason to say he has such a plan for us. I'm certain he cares about the decisions we make, but I'm certain that his main concern is the *kind* of decisions we make rather than *what* decisions we make. Imagine this conversation:

"Lord, I'm thinking of changing my job, and I was wondering what your will is in the matter."

"Tell me about it."

"Well, it's an honorable job and would mean more money. I would be able to support good works to a greater degree, and it would give my family some more security down the road."

"Well, that sounds good."

"On the other hand, it would mean more time away from my family, and I'd have to curtail some activities that I think are good for the church and the community."

"Well, you'll need to consider it carefully then, won't you?"

"Yes, that's why I've come to you, Lord. What do you think I should do?"

"Hmmm, what do you think you should do? It's up to you."

"You mean you aren't gong to help me decide, Lord? I'm going to have to do it by myself?"

"Of course not. I am helping you. Who do you think enables you to weigh these things? Who do you think has made you sensitive to different needs and commitments and how you should respond to them? I've been helping you make such decisions, even before this specific case came up."

"But what if I make the wrong decision? What if I don't make the choice you want me to make?"

"What makes you think I care which choice you make? You know I care about the *kind* of choice you make. But we're having this conversation because you wish to please me. That's all that matters."

"But Lord, what if the move turns out bad? Will you not keep me from making the wrong decision?"

216

"Sometimes I keep people from making 'wrong' decisions, but that's only in special cases. In this case, there is no 'wrong' decision. If things do work out 'bad,' that is, not as pleasant or as advantageous as it looks like they could, you and I will work it out together. In the meantime, your heart and mine are together in this—you want to please me, and I'm pleased that you do. So make your decision, and I'll work with you, whatever the result."

"Lord, this sounds as if you don't care what I do."

"Oh, that isn't true. Of course, I care what you do. If this were a choice between good and evil, we wouldn't be having this conversation. But it isn't. You're someone who wants to please me, and I'm telling you that it pleases me for you to make the choice that seems most pleasing to me as well as advantageous for you and others. I care about what makes you and your family happy, so if pleasing me and adding pleasure to your lives at the same time is an option, get on with it. As by my grace you grow in the image of Jesus Christ, your decision making will be purified and enriched, so I am always with you to help you make decisions."

◆

Set your heart to please me, and make whatever decision looks wisest and best. I'm content with that.

"But what if the decision I make is not your will?"

"You're assuming I have a preference in these matters. What makes you think that? Look, if I choose to hinder your move or prevent it, I'll do it. I'm quite capable of doing that, so you don't need to worry on that score. Where we aren't dealing with issues of good and evil, you set your heart to please me, and make whatever decision looks wisest and best to you. I'm content with that. Don't worry that you might decide something when I have already decided something else. You have no reason to think you might."

"Yes, but will you let me make a decision that would later bring pain? See, I'm asking you to keep me out of trouble."

"Oh, I thought we were talking about how to please me. If you're asking me to make sure you won't get hurt, that's a different thing altogether. I allow my people to make decisions that end up bringing them pain, so I won't undertake to keep you from that. I will and do help people make good decisions that very often keep them from heartache. But even good decisions might be costly."

"So, you have your moral and spiritual will, and you will help us discern it and live within it, but in all these other areas, you have no particular preference? I should simply weigh the pros and cons and get on with it?"

"That's about it. If I have any specific things I want done that require you to be at a given place at a given time to do a given thing, I'll get it done. No decision you make to please me can cause you ultimate loss. Not while I'm looking after you.

"But you'll find as you grow into my likeness that you'll not only think better, you'll think differently. Questions about houses, jobs, moves, investments, recreation, time management, felt needs, personal wishes, and other matters will become more important or less; categories will change places. The one thing that won't change, except for the better, is that you'll be seeking my reign and my righteousness. The rest is 'up for grabs.' "

"Well, how about if I make up my mind and give you the opportunity to close the door on it, if you wish. If you don't close the door, I will take it that you will it."

"If I wish to shut it down, I will. But I don't want you putting me on a timetable. Nor do I want you to claim I willed your purpose because it suited me to allow it. If you choose this action, you take responsibility for it. Don't say, 'God willed it.' "

And that's where the imaginary conversation ends. I think this is something like how we are to interact with God in these areas. I don't think there are any "nonmoral" areas in the life of a Christian. The nuts and bolts of our lives are parts of our lives as a whole, and the whole of our lives belong to God. I think all our decisions should be affected by our relationship with God.[1]

But this isn't the same as saying that God has our lives already mapped out in every detail and that we are to somehow find out what those details are so we won't do what's contrary to his will. Relax. Seek to please him by making decisions that are geared to honor him. It's more like bringing him our decisions to show him what we've done to please him than it is trying to figure out the blueprint and following it line by line.

We have freedom to make such choices. It isn't that the Spirit of God stands back and leaves us unaided. No, he works with us, shaping and transforming us into Christ's likeness, giving us wisdom through experience and so forth. The solution we come up with may be one of many possible solutions. And it's fine to say we believe that God helped us to this conclusion, as long as we're not giving the impression that he miraculously and infallibly guides us into every decision. Even biblical writings show a modesty when it comes to claiming to know God's will in the absence of clear and undoubted revelation.[2]

Buy the truth and do not sell it.

—Proverbs 23:23

✦

Musings on Truth and Tolerance

Can the existence of different churches be explained by saying that they had arguments over doctrine? Yes, but many major religious movements and their branches arose as a result of political and cultural upheavals rather than doctrinal disagreement.[1]

What about those that do stand apart because of doctrinal differences? Is it legitimate for people to stand apart over how they view religious, biblical, or theological truth? I don't see why not. We think it's legitimate in many areas—politics, social reform, the sciences, and so forth. No one thinks this strange, and we shouldn't think it strange in the religious realm.

Almost as bad as "insiders" dividing over trivial matters are "outsiders" who sneer or snarl and call all differences "trivia." In doing this, they ignore the sincerity and earnestness of those who really want to please God and serve humanity, to say nothing of the biblical witness. I think, at one and the same time, that we make too little and too much out of the existence of different churches.[2]

In the political arena, "liberals" and "conservatives" stand against each other because they think the differences are basic enough to require it. Millions cast their votes with passion for and against, and woe to anyone who declares it all paltry. Political parties agree on many basic things, don't they? Like caring for the poor and needy, democracy as opposed to anarchy, free market rather than a rugged socialism, and so forth. But for all their agreements (and ignoring some outright foolishness), they stand apart for reasons that seem right to them.

The jeering or snarling outsider wants to say that differing believers hate each other or that what they differ on is invariably trivia. It's true that there are some believers who give grounds for the critic's frustration, but no credit is given to those millions who differ without ugliness and draw some lines where they think large issues are at stake.

The critical outsiders wouldn't be able to stomach what follows, though the chances of them reading it are slim indeed. But maybe those who hold that religious convictions are—to say the least—as important as other matters will find something useful here.

We all have to "call it as we see it." In our search to know, do, and teach the will of God for our lives, it's right to depend on others who are more experienced, devoted, and gifted than we are—but we're to give our hearts and minds to no one but the Lord.

However we reach our conclusions (even if it's that we don't know which one to draw), we must call it as we see it.

This is how it should be. No one should want us to simply parrot their conclusions. They shouldn't want us to surrender our intellectual integrity. But shouldn't we want the same thing for them? Even if it were possible to bully or bribe people into our camp, in the end, we'd be ashamed of them and ourselves—or should be. More ashamed of ourselves, I hope, because we used the fears and longings of vulnerable people to keep them from maintaining their inner integrity.

Where we feel compelled to differ, it'll be because we think we *should* differ in order to please God. We'll differ because that's how we are hearing the Word of God at present. It won't be because we "don't like" one another or because my aunt had a bad experience with your group or some such thing. In the spirit of Luther, we'll say, "Here we stand, God help us, we can do no other."

It's interesting that while we all draw circles that exclude others, it's when we're on the receiving end of the exclusion order that we're hacked off. When we do it, it's a matter of conscience; when others do it, it's bad manners, an ugly spirit, or just plain bigotry. Maybe we all need to be more charitable to one another, whichever end we're on.

I won't stop to establish that there are teachings which the New Testament views as jugular. See the passages cited in the endnotes that show this is so.[3]

✦

However we reach our conclusions, we all have to call it as we see it.

Now, it's true that some of us hold one thing to be jugular and others think it's not; but even here we're going to have to call it as we see it. This much is clear, the higher we raise the stakes, the more certain we'll want to be about our grounds for calling it jugular.

223

Two of us might agree that the issue we're differing on, while not without importance, is also not a life-or-death matter. We'll want to be right on the subject, of course, but if we think it isn't a matter of life or death, the stakes are considerably lowered. What's not a test of salvation in Christ must not be regarded as jugular!

But even the major doctrines of the Christian faith can he held in an ungodly spirit. It's clear there is one God, but to sneer at those who don't hold that view isn't the fruit of biblical monotheism. Paul argues from monotheism that all humans are loved by God, that none is excluded, and that his grace is available to them all. This is the opposite of sneering and smugness.[4]

Haven't you noticed that a man with a gentle and Christlike spirit can have "narrow" views, to which we may strenuously object, yet we aren't eager to go to war with him? Another man with a sneering and bullying manner really hacks us off, even if he's broader theologically. Why is this the case? Part of the answer seems obvious to me. We simply find obnoxious people hard to bear—whatever their views—and those with a genuinely sweet spirit warm us even while we're disagreeing. Perhaps we who hold our doctrinal convictions with great passion can bear this in mind.

If we do arrive at a point where we believe we must draw a circle that excludes others from our fellowship:

- We'll call it that way because it looks that way to us. If we have any doubts about it, we won't draw the excluding circle, and we won't allow others to bully us into drawing it.

- We'll do it after we've made a thorough examination of the biblical witness in the matter. We won't place a conviction in the jugular category unless we've done our biblical homework. We won't stand apart until we think we've indisputable grounds for standing together; rather, we'll stand together until we think we've indisputable grounds for standing apart.

- We'll do it with sadness, because we find no joy in it; with humility, knowing we're not God's pets; with gentleness, because that's how Christ is.

- We'll do it with the clear understanding that we aren't infallible and that later study might lead us to change our views. (Some of us can easily confess that we make mistakes in numerous areas but find it hard to admit we could be mistaken in biblical interpretation.)

- We'll do it with the glad confession that God is the only sovereign, that even our correct judgment is always open to his veto, and that he is free to act as he wills. He is no prisoner to his biblical laws, though he can never be untrue to himself.

The elect of God are to bear witness to the truth God has entrusted to them, they have no other option—and what's more, they don't apologize for having no other. They must exclude from their fellowship certain people, however noble and fine those people are (not to mention those who will not submit to the truth of God in behavior or teaching). But the elect of God will not proceed to tell God what he can or cannot do, either now or hereafter!

Whatever else we do, if we wish to image Christ, we'll maintain a sweet spirit. If for reasons that seem good to you, you reluctantly draw a circle that excludes me from fellowship, I should give you credit for trying to please God. If I draw a circle that excludes you, you should credit me with the same purpose. We'll rejoice in all the truths we share and let God make the final call.

225

Keeping God's commands is what counts.

—1 Corinthians 7:19

✦

Truth Is for Doing

As I write this piece, I'm weary and temporarily bummed out. The reasons aren't relevant, only the feeling and mood. I had thought to leave the writing until I'm over it, but the more I think of it, the more I'm persuaded I should write now. Countless people, as a consequence of their unchanging dismal circumstances, days without end, feel as I do right now, and perhaps I'm in the position to feel a little of what they so often feel about the "be ye warmed and filled" kind of speech. I'm not planning to carefully nuance any of what follows. You're going to have to do that for yourself.

So this surgeon tells his colleague that the man's toes have turned gangrenous and if something isn't done quickly, it'll spread to his feet. His friend says, "Well, you'd better tell him and get on with the amputation."

The surgeon says, "But he likes me. I've developed a good rapport with him, and I don't want to spoil it by giving him bad news and then cutting off his toes. I was thinking of trying vitamins and getting him to watch comedy movies. Lots of studies have proved that laughing stimulates the immune system and energizes the body's recovery powers. I'd just hate to take the unpleasant route and have him mad at me."

We all want to try the "positive" approach. It offends fewer people and doesn't give the impression that we're unbending and negative. The positive approach makes sense, if it's honorable and works, but sometimes it takes a lot of plain talk and foul-tasting medicine to effect a cure.

Truth is for doing! Truth is for doing at a personal, ethical level; it's for doing in the presence of the poor and needy; it's for doing in the company of the emotional basket cases whose hearts are fragmented. It's for doing at a congregational level when power struggles flair; it's for doing before a world that's in awful need of seeing and hearing the gospel of salvation and reconciliation.

Truth's not for admiring, reading, defending, writing, or reciting; it's not for memorizing, analyzing, teaching, or preaching; it's not for debating, writing, singing, or spreading—it's for doing!

> Dear children, do not let anyone lead you astray. He who *does* what is right is righteous, just as he is righteous.[1]

> If we say that we have fellowship with him and walk in the darkness, we lie, and *do* not the truth.[2]

> If anyone has material possessions and sees his brother in need but has no pity on him, how can the love of God be

in him? Dear children, let us not love with words or tongue but with *actions* and in truth.[3]

Everything about 1 John stresses the need to do what is true. The writings of Luke are saturated with the call to do. Over and over again, he frames the issues like this: "What shall we do?" "What must we do?" "What do you want me to do?" "He will tell you what you must do!" "What must I do?" "Go and do likewise." "Do this and live."

The Christ said to the apostolic group, after teaching them, "Now that you know these things, you will be blessed if you *do* them."[4] He said the difference between a wise and a foolish man was not in the hearing but in the doing of his word.[5] James spoke of being doers rather than forgetful hearers.[6]

We're able to give ten thousand reasons why we shouldn't be held to obeying God's truth in areas involving business integrity, sexual purity, forgiving those who sin against us, the use of wealth, racism, family abuse (parental or child), congregational division, loyalty, resentment, seizing power, demanding of rights, showing compassion, or submitting to biblical ordinances. Tell people sexual promiscuity is out, and somebody mutters, "Legalist." Say it's sin to dump your husband or wife and move in with somebody else, and a textual debate begins. Say that God wills our holiness,[7] and somebody wants discussions about "changing cultures." Say we need to band together to save crumbling families, and we're sure to hear about the possibility of being sued.

It seems no truth is plain until we have forty theologians armed with degrees in historical, form, source, sociological, rhetorical, and constructionist criticism. Our speech can become so lawyerlike and slick that if we used it on the wrong side of the law, we'd earn ourselves five years hard time. The result is like fireworks in a fog, and even some of the experts, in a daze, looking at their colleagues, finally throw up their hands and walk off disgusted. They finally see themselves as word merchants, peddling their wares while a world burns and a church, with more than amnesia, loses its way.

We enjoy a hermeneutic of tolerance. Yes, we know what the passage demands, but beyond that, what will it let us get away with?

"I honestly believe we can get by with a lot less theology," said the angry Colin Morris, "provided the little we need is all used up."[8] Morris was a leader in the British Methodist movement when a Zambian immigrant died of hunger not far from Morris's front door. The man's sole possessions were the shorts and ragged shirt he wore and an empty ballpoint pen. When they examined him, he had a ball of grass in his stomach.

Colin exploded and wrote, "Your theology, fancy or plain, is what you are when the talking stops and the action begins," and he offered to sell his vote to any side on any issue in the Anglican-Methodist unity meeting, provided they sent eight dollars to some charity that fed the poor.

Increasingly, we gather at our joy-filled conferences, sing happy songs, and listen to generic truths without teeth and interesting new insights to old texts. We're made to laugh at our apathy rather than repent of it, we fall in the aisles giggling while the church that nurtured our faith is made to look foolish, and we go back home feeling higher than a kite.

In our jubilant mood, we neither understand nor care to understand, the dismay, anger, frustration, or panic in people—people like "Elizabeth," whose very mind is coming unglued under the prolonged pressure of a chaotic home! We know what's going on, but won't band together to do something about it.

"What can we do?"

What do we want to do?

God comes to our assembly as Elizabeth, and we offer him a few words of advice, sympathetic sounds, grave nods of the head, and we go back to our happy songs, sermon preparation, or golf swing.

If we'd known it was God who came to our assembly, we would have treated him better. It *was* God who came to our assembly! And "inasmuch as you didn't do it unto her, you didn't do it unto me."

Truth is for doing! And if our assemblies were less like comedy hours with a floor show thrown in, if we came together to "rejoice with trembling" at the thought that God will lay more *doing* truths on our hearts, maybe people like Elizabeth would survive in greater numbers, and maybe little men with empty ballpoint pens in their pockets and grass in their bellies wouldn't die near our front doors.

◆

If we'd known it was God who came to our assembly, we would have treated him better.

There's something crazy about it all, like some sort of nutty theater play. On one end, we have those who care only about doctrinal correctness (that is, one or two points of adored truth—the rest don't seem to matter— least of all that truth about loving brothers and sisters). Beyond that, they do nothing to bring the gospel to the lost or get involved in social pain. On the other end of the spectrum are those who care less and less about plain truth, unless it's the kind that provides for their happiness and doesn't ask them to do a lot. The one end muzzles all truth but the couple of points they want to straitjacket everyone with. The other end doesn't want to hear any truth that might diminish their right to feel good about themselves while they're being blessed.

THERE IS TRUTH

Some of us, foaming at the mouth in our dwindling churches are hurling verbal and paper missiles. Others of us are majestically and "maturely" ignoring the bigots, as we entertain ourselves with happy truths, happy songs, and inspirational books. Meanwhile, Elizabeth and a nameless little man with an empty ballpoint pen slip silently into oblivion.

But in either case, it's the old word game again. We know we're vitally concerned about Elizabeth and the man with no name, because we keep on and on saying so. We love nothing better than to work through another "issue," listen to one more entertaining and well-polished delivery, or sing another stanza of a joy-bringing song. Talk, talk, and more talk! No wonder Albert Schweitzer, after twenty years of reading and talking in theology and philosophy, went off and buried himself in Africa where he could do good without having to say anything.

By the time we've argued or sung ourselves to exhaustion, we've nothing left to give to the God in a ragged shirt with grass in his belly. We're like the bar owner who's never open for business because he keeps drinking his stock. We gorge ourselves on life-saving truths and can't feel the hunger of others.

And it might not be so bad if we were putting out profound truths that empower us to face life bravely and in a costly way, but we're saying the same narrow and banal things over and over again. The wild joy of a prospector who finds pure gold after excavating an entire mountain is no greater than the ecstasy of the average Christian who sees in the ever-rolling stream of verbiage a single profound sentence that was worth the effort.

"Professor X has just rewritten his book," said a weary reviewer, and that just about covers most of what we're writing. It could equally be, "Minister X has just preached his series of sermons again." Those of us who feel we've been called to speak and/or write are required to offer the whole counsel of God so as to enable and inspire people to truth. But so much of what we offer is not creative theology; it's the endless parroting and squawking of the same fossilized interpretations—interpretations that keep disciples from thrusting deep into enemy territory to rescue others and instead drive them there to their own demise.

Then we react in dismay when the world (and some weary disciples), bored with our patter, walks away saying, "To hell with you!" That may or may not be of any consequence, but they often add, "and to hell with your Jesus as well!" Now that is a matter of consequence.

Truth is for doing, whatever our place in life is. And God has made it clear that he wearies of people who, as a policy, treat it as a commodity we store up in case we might one day need it for something or other.

"Make it your aim to do what is right. . . . See that justice prevails. . . . Stop your noisy songs; I do not want to listen to your harps. Instead, let justice flow like a stream, and righteousness like a river that never goes dry."[9]

In the way of righteousness there is life;
along that path is immortality.
—Proverbs 12:28

✦

No Dead End!

Frank Boreham and a couple of friends took the road north simply because they'd never done it before.[1] They walked for a very long time, and though it seemed it would never end, they stuck to it, looking for something special. A posh car roared by them when they had been a long time into their trudge, but in only a few moments it returned the way it had come.

The friends understood why about thirty minutes later when they saw the fence that stretched all the way across the road—it was a dead end! No wonder the car had come back so quickly.

Imagine the conversation that evening at supper—as the high-brows ate their fish or nibbled on after-dinner mints—about how they had wasted all that time driving up a road leading nowhere.

THERE IS TRUTH

Fancy that. Still, at least they were in a car, not like those poor walkers who would have to plod all the way back to wherever they'd come from. And wouldn't that have triggered someone (probably one of the ladies) to say in good-natured sympathy, "Poor things"?

What they couldn't have known as they pushed their chairs back from the dinner table and talked of roads that led nowhere—what they couldn't have known was this: When Boreham and his friends climbed the fence and walked a couple of hundred yards, past some trees and over the brow of the hill, they found paradise—a valley that simply stunned them to silence with its beauty. Below them lay a silver, winding river with gorgeous willow trees lining its banks, bending over, their branches often dipping into the water, giving vitality and movement to it as they broke the lazy surface. Green fields and flowers stretched as far as the eye could see, and larks were doing graceful gymnastics as they chased each other through the blue sky and over the surface of the river. As if to cap it all off, a kingfisher settled on a tree less than thirty feet from them—parading his lovely blue plumage, snow white throat, and nut brown head—eyeing the humans with tolerance and interest.

Those who retired to the reading room had mistaken an obstacle for a "dead end." Their good-natured sympathy, had they known it, should have been for themselves.

God help us, so often we give up too soon. We don't persevere, can't see it through, feel it's too much of a challenge. There's nothing beyond; we've come to the end of the road, and it led nowhere.

There was Israel, under threat from Assyria, looking down from the walls only to gape at menacing troops as far as the eye could see, only to watch the foreign engineers examining the walls, figuring how best to bring them down. There was the king, going around the walls consoling the people, dressed in dull garments that spoke of mourning and repentance rather than the glory and color of God's regent.

But God's word through the prophet Isaiah assured them that they hadn't come to the end of a road leading nowhere. Before he was through, the alien armies would vanish from the land and the king would be dressed again in his finery. This is how he puts it: "Your eyes will see the king in his beauty and view a land that stretches afar."[2]

And don't you remember poor Peter's hot outburst, "I'm going fishing!"? A dead end, a road that led nowhere. But when morning came, someone on the beach was telling them where to throw their nets if they wanted a big catch. That familiar voice, that familiar advice, and paradise opened up before them.[3]

Then there were Christ's lovely lady-friends, who went to care for his body that Sunday morning and were beside themselves with grief because he wasn't where they'd laid him.[4] A dead end? A road going nowhere?

Hardly. If they had found him where they'd laid him, now that would have been the end! But in their grief, a familiar voice speaks, and a whole new world begins for them.

Everywhere we look, we're confronted with fences—right across our paths: long years of work, an assembly that's no better off for our having been there, a failed marriage, useless educational degrees, a search for justice stymied, a brutal rape, unjustly fired from the job, an economic slump and layoffs, wayward children, hospital bills, and savings wiped out—dead ends. After all this time and effort, the road led nowhere.

But are you sure? Can that really be? In a world into which Christ himself came, offering life to the full?[5] If the Story is the truth, can dismay be permanent? Do we need to shake our heads in despair for anyone—ourselves or others? If the love of God sent him, if the love of God came in him, surely all that is right and fair and generous will be done in the end. And no one in all the world need fear—whoever they are—that the wrongs will not be righted.

And if our Story's true, if he lives triumphant, then the grave is not the end; an endlessly silent, lightless, frozen universe is not the final scene. Then there is no dead end! Praise God, there is no dead end! The end will be as he wants it to be, will be what holiness and generosity and faithfulness make it to be.

How sad it is, then, when people glance at him and turn from him without looking closely. Turn away thinking there's nothing much there, all stories and no substance. "He promised to be the way to a better life, a better world, a richer, fuller joy; but when we gave him the once-over, he turned out to be a dead end. No, we're wasting our time with him. Back to the car, back to the library and the after-dinner mints. Back to counting the days as oblivion approaches."

No, our Story is true! No, this is no dead end. Some of us have heard the Story of what's beyond the fence, so we head toward it with a spring in our step. Some of us have already climbed the fence and are enjoying paradise and know the full proof that this Christ of ours is the Way, the Truth, and the Life.

So, however difficult it is for you who are poor and weary and heartsick on the journey, do it anyway—climb the fence, just get over this one, scramble up the bank between the trees, and look, expecting paradise; for one of these days that's what you'll see. And when you do, you'll look back at your friends who linger in doubt and you'll call to them, "Come and see. I told you it was no dead end!"

Notes

Introduction:
ESCAPING THE SPIRIT?

1. Ps. 139:7–12. The psalmist seems to be half-complaining, but in the end, quite relieved.

2. *The Pure in Heart* (London: Epworth Press, 1955), 50.

3. If you want some serious works that will show how central the doctrine of the Spirit is in New Testament life and literature, you might want to consult James Dunn's *Jesus and the Spirit* and Max Turner's *Power from on High* (dealing with Luke/Acts) and Gordon Fee's *God's Empowering Presence* (a study of the Spirit in Paul's letters). Be sure to also consult the major articles in various encyclopedias.

Chapter One. Where the Spirit of the Lord Is . . .
THERE IS TRANSFORMATION

The Spirit and Mr. Hyde

1. 2 Cor. 3:18 ASV.
2. Rom. 8:18–24.

Of Pigs and Ancient Magic

1. The story is told in Homer's *Odyssey,* bk. 10. See *Harvard Classics,* edited by C. W. Eliot. Danbury, Conn.: Grolier Enterprises Corp., or Robert Graves, *The Greek Myths* (Middlesex, England: Penguin Books, 1969), 2:358–9.
2. Hos. 11:8 TEV.
3. 2 Pet. 3:9.
4. Luke 18:9–14.
5. Luke 10:30–32.

Nightingales in Berkeley Square

1. Isa. 10:5–7.
2. Isa. 8:22.
3. Isa. 32:12–14.
4. Isa. 32:15.
5. Isa. 35:1–2, 6–7.
6. Written by Eric Maschwitz and Manning Sherwin, 1930s.
7. Isa. 44:2–3.

Beauty and the Beast

1. 1 Pet. 4:8.
2. Matt. 18:10–20.

The Wind of the Spirit

1. Quoted in Sangster, *The Pure in Heart* , 51.
2. Ps. 22:1.
3. Ps. 22:2.
4. Ps. 22:3–5.
5. Ps. 22:6–8.
6. Ezek. 37:1–14.
7. Ps. 22:24.
8. Ps. 22:25.
9. Ps. 22:30–31.

He Did It for Others; He Can Do It for You!

1. Luke 4:18-19.
2. 1 Cor. 6:9-11.
3. Sangster, *Pure in Heart,* xi.
4. Gal. 5:17 RSV.
5. 1 John 4:4; John 16:33.

Elephant Men

1. Luke 2:52; Acts 2:47; 16:2; and elsewhere.
2. Rom. 16:1–2; 1 Cor. 16:3; 2 Cor. 8:18–19.
3. Acts 4:19–20; see 5:29.
4. 1 Cor. 9:1–3.
5. 1 Cor. 4:3.
6. Acts 26:17 paraphrased.
7. The movie is based on *The Elephant Man; A Study in Human Dignity* by Ashley Montagu and the recollections of Dr. Frederick Treves. Everyone should be *forced* to watch the movie. If they want to.
8. Prior's great little book deserves to be better known. It's called

The Suffering and the Glory (London: Hodder & Stoughton, 1985), 109–10.

    9. Rom. 5:5.

    10. Luke 15:17.

What Is Christ Prepared to Do?

    1. Quoted in Lord Guthrie's *Robert Louis Stevenson* (Edinburgh: W. Green & Son, 1924), 15. I once said this remark of Stevenson's was addressed to his father. A writer misled me.

    2. From the movie *The Untouchables,* starring Kevin Costner, Sean Connery, and Robert De Niro. This is a two-thumbs-up, six-fingers-down type movie.

Chapter Two. Where the Spirit of the Lord Is . . .
THERE IS GLORY FOR CHRIST

The Spirit and Center Stage

    1. John 16:14.

    2. Take thirty minutes to glance through the preaching in the Book of Acts and notice the centrality of Jesus Christ in all they said.

    3. See, for example, Heb. 3:1 and 12:2–3 and the unending appeal to the person and work of Christ throughout the New Testament writings.

    4. Since the Spirit is part of the Godhead, how could we not be called to give him full honor? And how could we not be enriched by watching this divine Person at work?

    5. While it is most certainly not inappropriate to worship and glorify the Spirit, it is important to listen to what he teaches us in this regard. In the Scriptures, praise is rarely directed expressly to the Spirit, even though worship takes place "in" and "through" him. See what I

mean by reading through praise sections of the Bible. The psalms are especially revealing in this matter, and in the New Testament we have sections like Rev. 4:9–11; 5:9–14; 7:9–14. I mention all this simply to say that it is no new role of the Spirit to "take a back seat."

Led by the Spirit

1. 1 Cor. 12:3.
2. Ibid.
3. 1 Cor. 8:6.
4. John 16:13.
5. John 16:14.

Jesus Is Lord!

1. Luke 10:17–21.
2. Acts 5:41; 2 Cor. 12:9; Phil. 1:18.
3. 1 Cor. 8:6; Eph. 4:4–6.

I Saw a Butterfly

1. 2 Cor. 4:6–7.
2. Eph. 3:21.
3. Jer. 9:23–24; quoted by Paul in 1 Cor. 1:31 and 2 Cor. 10:17.
4. See, for example, Acts 4:8–12, 31. To be filled with despair is to have nothing in us but a deep sense of hopelessness. At that moment we have so much in us that it has to come out, in word or look or tone, and it comes out as brokenness and loss. If we're filled with rage or bitterness or compassion or booze, we act or speak in rage, bitterness, compassion, or drunkenness. We're under the influence or control of the things with which we're filled, though that moment may/will pass. To be filled with the Spirit is to act at that time under the Spirit's sway. And see how being filled with the Spirit

affects character and behavior in general: Acts 4:36–37; 9:26–27; 11:22–24.

5. Rev. 5:12.

Wistful Unbelievers

1. Mark 6:4.

2. Frank Boreham has the record of this in his *The Luggage of Life* (London: Epworth Press, 1927), 56.

3. 1 Tim. 1:16.

Shaping the Christ

1. The Greek text has "eternal spirit." I think we're certainly right to follow those who understand this to be the Holy Spirit. If that is true, the Spirit of God enabled Jesus to be the spotless sacrifice.

2. The Greek text has only "holy spirit."

3. Luke 1:35 and the inferential conjunction, *dio*.

4. Luke 2:52.

5. See Luke 4:1–2; Isa. 63:10–14; John Nolland, *Word Biblical Commentary*, 35a (Dallas: Word, 1989), 178; and Max Turner, *Power from on High* (Sheffield, England: Sheffield Academic Press, 1996), 204.

6. Phil. 2:5–11.

The World He Came to Save

1. Isa. 42:1–4. There's a play on words between what the Servant will not do and what he will not experience. See verse 4.

2. Luke 12:32, paraphrased.

3. Quoted in *The Best Loved Poems of the American People* (New York: Doubleday, 1936), 88–89.

This Christ Is King!

1. Acts 2:36, paraphrased; 10:36; 1 Pet. 3:22.
2. Acts 16:12.
3. Phil. 2:7–11.
4. Acts 17:7.
5. Quoted in N. T. Wright's *What Saint Paul Really Said* (Grand Rapids, Mich.: Eerdmans, 1997), 43.
6. Gerhard Kittel, ed., *Theological Dictionary of the New Testament* (Grand Rapids, Mich.: Eerdmans, 1971), 2:721–35.
7. I've developed this a little more in *Jesus, Hero of Thy Soul* (West Monroe, La.: Howard Publishing Co.), 47–53.

Every Hair on My Head

1. Luke 4:17–19.
2. Acts 10:38.
3. The incident is rehearsed in Frank Boreham's *Dreams at Sunset* (London: Epworth Press, 1956), 61.

Chapter Three. *Where the Spirit of the Lord Is . . .* THERE IS FREEDOM

Truth and Emotions

1. Gal. 5:1.
2. Rom. 8:2.

Free Because Forgiven

1. Luke 7:36–50, especially 42, 43, 47.
2. Rom. 3:22–23.
3. In *Pilgrim's Progress* by John Bunyan.

4. A. C. Armstrong, *The Forgiveness of Sins* (n.p.: New York, 1905), 1–25.

5. Isa. 6:1–8.

6. Ps. 51:12–14.

7. Isa. 63:8.

8. Isa. 63:9.

9. The story line is from the movie *The Mission*, starring Robert De Niro and Jeremy Irons.

Free from Meaningless Pain

1. 2 Cor. 5:7. C. K. Barrett and others, but see Ralph Martin on this passage and Arndt and Gingrich on *eidos*, page 221.

2. 2 Cor. 3:4, 6; 4:1.

3. 2 Cor. 4:1, 16.

4. 2 Cor. 4:16–18.

5. 2 Cor. 1:3–4, 8–10.

6. The atheist J. N. Findlay, in his contribution to *New Essays in Philosophical Theology* (New York: Macmillan, 1964), 75, concluded his offering with this candid remark: "I am not at all keen to shake faiths or overturn altars (if indeed I were able to do so)." This he said after saying that the falsehood of Christianity makes a better world than the truth of atheism. Contrast that with 2 Cor. 3:12–13 and 10:4–5 where Paul sees himself at war and prepared to overturn "altars" and shake faiths.

7. 2 Cor. 4:13, paraphrased.

Free from Legalism

1. I think it is important that we be careful about labeling people "legalists." It isn't legalism to be slow to change our views or to hold our convictions passionately. This may be a sign of maturity and health rather than legalism. And we shouldn't think all "legal-

ists" are equally legalistic. Some people are quite bald, others are very bald, and still others are utterly bald. So it is with "liberals" and "legalists."

2. 1 Cor. 7:19.

3. Ps. 119:97.

4. Zeph. 3:14–18; see Isa. 62:5.

5. *A Captive Voice: The Liberation of Preaching* (Louisville, Ky.: Westminster Press, 1994), 46–47.

6. *The Waiting Father* (Greenwood, S.C.: The Attic Press, Inc., 1978), 129.

7. Rom. 8:1–2. I'm not pretending to explain this text, only to rejoice in it.

Free to Say No to Freedom

1. 2 Cor. 3:17.

2. 2 Cor. 5:14 NEB; see 1 Cor. 9:16–17.

3. 1 Cor. 9:19.

4. Rom. 5:5.

5. Exod. 21:1–6.

6. *The Highway of God* (Edinburgh: T&T Clark, 1931), 187–8.

7. The whole story is told in 2 Sam. 13–15.

8. See John 6:66–69.

Free from Abusive Emotions

1. Luke 4:18–19.

2. I certainly think it's true that some people need professional help and that we should use this help as one of the ways God rescues us! I also think that Paul Tournier is right when he says that most of what is effective in the work of professionals can be given to us by wise and committed friends in Christ.

3. Luke 15, see esp. verses 1–10, 21–24, 31–32.

4. Words and music by Bernard of Clairveaux, Edward Caswall, and John B. Dykes.

Free from Anxiety

1. Luke 12:32.
2. Luke 12:4.
3. Luke 12:11.
4. Luke 12:4, 7, 11, 22, 32.
5. Luke 12:30, paraphrased.
6. Luke 9:1–2; 10:1, 9, 17, 21–24; Matt. 12:27.
7. Luke 12:33–34.
8. Luke 12:25–26. But Christ would never have dreamed of denying that fear can be healthy and that it can move us to be creative and to escape.
9. See a Greek lexicon on *eudokesen.*
10. Luke 12:24, 28.
11. Luke 11:13.
12. Luke 12:31.
13. Matt. 12:28; 2 Cor. 1:22; Eph. 1:14.
14. Gal. 5:22–23.
15. Luke 10:17.
16. Luke 10:21.
17. Luke 10:20.

Free from Pretense

1. See 2 Cor. 2:16; 3:4–6.
2. 2 Cor. 4:7 KJV.
3. 2 Cor. 1:8–9.
4. *The Second Epistle to the Corinthians* (London: A&C Black, 1990), 66.
5. 2 Cor. 3:5, paraphrased.

Chapter Four: Where the Spirit of the Lord Is . . .
THERE IS LOVE

The Fruit of the Spirit Is . . .

1. Rom. 6:23; Eph. 1:3.
2. Rom. 8:29. Note that even here, the stress is not on our loveliness but on Christ's glory. "That he might be the firstborn among many brothers."
3. Phil. 1:6.
4. 2 Cor. 1:22. See the lexicons on the word used.
5. *Jesus and the Spirit* (Philadelphia: Westminster Press, 1975), 294.
6. See, for example, Gal. 3:1–5, 21; 5:14, 22–25; and Rom. 8:1–4.

Where It Pleases

1. Rom. 1:18–32.
2. Rom. 2:14–15, 26.
3. Rom. 3:9–20.
4. John 3:8.
5. John 3:1–8.
6. The point of Gal. 5:13–25 is not to say that only Christians can manifest the fruit of the Spirit. It is to say Christians should produce no other fruit. Division and immorality, he says, are not the fruit of the Spirit. You can recognize those who are under the Spirit's influence, for their way of life will show his presence.

The Bookkeeper Is Dead

1. Lev. 19:18.
2. The whole story is worthy of a number of readings. Don't let the dated style put you off.

Love Isn't Touchy

1. *Respectable Sins* (London: Hodder & Stoughton, 1909). I've borrowed from Watson in this section and in what follows. I also find Harry E. Fosdick's *On Being a Real Person* (London: SCM Press, 1943) readable and challenging in this area. Much of the advice and guidance given about this whole matter is either too obvious to merit development or little more than a description of the problem. At least, that's how it appears to me.
2. 1 Cor. 13:5.
3. Rom. 15:16; 1 Cor. 6:11.

Love Protects

1. Rom. 4:18.
2. *Greek-English Lexicon of the New Testament and Other Early Christian Literature,* 2nd ed. (Chicago: Chicago University Press, 1979), 765–6.
3. Matt. 18:1–20, esp. v. 15. This whole chapter is about the importance of every person. See verses 6, 10–14. It isn't about "the proper way to get rid of a sinner."
4. The story is rehearsed in *The Speaker's Bible,* vol. 2, bk. 2 (Grand Rapids, Mich.: Baker Book House, 1978), 88.
5. Job 6:14, "A despairing man should have the devotion of his friends, even though he forsakes the fear of the Almighty."

God's Bundle and Ours

1. 1 John 4:11.
2. 1 John 4:10, 19.
3. Rom. 5:5. It's an open question with me whether this passage speaks of God's love for us or ours for him. The point remains the same.

Lord of All or Not Lord at All

1. Matt. 22:38.
2. Matt. 10:34–39; Luke 14:25–33.
3. John 12:21.

Love Rejoices

1. *The Way* (New York: Doubleday, 1978), 265.
2. Matt. 22:30; 1 Cor. 6:13.
3. Ps. 104:10–15, 21, 27–30.
4. Luke 10:20.
5. Isa. 65:19; Zeph. 3:17.
6. Neh. 8:1–10; and see Rom. 15:13.
7. *Flesh and Spirit* (Nashville: Abingdon; London: SCM Press, 1962), 82.

Love and Peace of Mind

1. Matt. 26:37–38 NEB.
2. See 1 Thess. 2:17–3:8. When Paul's Thessalonian friends came under attack and he had lost contact with them, he worried about them. When he couldn't wait any longer in ignorance, he sent Timothy to see how they fared. Timothy came back with grand news for Paul and his companions, and Paul said, "Now we really live." (See how the different versions render this phrase from 3:8.) The worry, the unbearable silence, had deprived them of that fullness of life and made them feel as though they weren't really living. The reports of persecution drifted back, the fear of the Thessalonians falling away entered their hearts, but the great news of their faith restored life to Paul and his companions. Paul isn't apologizing here for his concern, he's proclaiming it.
3. 2 Cor. 11:28.

Chapter Five. Where the Spirit of the Lord Is . . .
THERE IS COMMUNITY

We're Something Else

1. Gen. 1.
2. Rom. 8:18–21; 1 Cor. 15:44–49.
3. Eph. 2:14–18.
4. Eph. 4:11–16.
5. Heb. 10:24–25 PHILLIPS.

Weeping in the Aisles

1. Eph. 4:1–6, esp. vv. 1–3.
2. Gal. 3:26–28 RSV.
3. See Gen. 11:1–9.
4. 2 Cor. 1:20.

To Eat or Not to Eat?

1. Rom. 7:1; 11:13; and elsewhere.
2. *Kosher,* meaning "fit" (to eat). But the debate might also have been between Gentiles who had come out of an idolatrous background. See 1 Cor. 8–10.
3. Not even non-Christian Jews took that position.
4. Gal. 2:3–5 where circumcision was a salvation issue and Acts 16:3 where it wasn't. Many today would be willing to say that "social drinkers" were sinning in supporting the booze industry but would not be willing to say it was a life-or-death issue.
5. Rom. 14:1–2, 14; see 1 Cor. 8:7–8.
6. Rom. 14:14, 23.
7. Rom. 8:32.
8. Rom. 6:1–6, 17–18; 14:4.

9. Rom. 14:7.

10. Rom. 14:17.

11. Rom. 14:20–21 with 1 Cor. 8:9–11. The passage, I'm sure, speaks directly to someone who sins by eating against his conscience, but its thrust would also embrace encouraging him to sin in other ways. A stubborn and ungracious eater could provoke the noneater into dividing the assembly.

12. 1 Cor. 8:13, slightly paraphrased.

13. Rom. 14:17.

Love Will Find a Way

1. The whole story is told in 2 Sam. 13–14. 2 Sam. 14:14 is riddled with difficulties both textual and exegetical. See how the various versions translate it. What the great majority of them agree on is this: God is in favor of reconciliation, whether it is he or other lovers of people who devise the means.

2. Words and music by John Lennon, from the album *The John Lennon Collection,* copyright belongs to Lenono Music/BMG Music Publishing LTD, 1980.

Sunday Morning

1. 1 Cor. 11:25–26.

Some Anti-Class Remarks

1. I wouldn't want to deny that the Bible is rich in psychological insights, and I certainly believe that some truths of psychology can give us insight into scriptures. Nor would I wish to deny that we should take advantage of every bit of this. I am wanting to say that the Bible was not written as a key to emotional health and happiness, and I believe that viewing it as though it were does the Community of Faith serious injury.

2. To say that the discussion of "needs" should never enter into our relationship with God and one another is nonsense. But the issue I'm focusing on here is how our needs are to be viewed and met, especially when it involves how we view and structure assemblies.

3. This is where the work of people like Stanley Hauerwas is so important. His emphasis (with others) on character formation is so important and so constructive.

4. See Ray Fulenwider's *The Servant-Driven Church* (Joplin: College Press, 1998) to balance what's been said here.

The Outer Fringe

1. 1 Cor. 12:23.
2. Gal. 5:25.

On Our Side of the Gulf

1. Ezra 9:6 MOFFATT.
2. Dan. 9:4–19.
3. Acts 2:23.
4. The quotation is found in H. R. Mackintosh's *The Christian Experience of Forgiveness* (London: Nisbet & Co, 1927), 214.
5. *The Meaning of the Cross* (London: Hodder & Stoughton, 1931), 170.

Chapter 6. Where the Spirit of the Lord Is . . .
THERE IS TRUTH

Truth and the Believer

1. Luke 10:25–28.

Camel and Gnats

1. Phil. 2:5–11; 1 Cor. 12:3.
2. Matt. 12:28–29; Luke 4:14; 9:51; 16–21; 22:42; John 3:16–17.
3. 1 Cor. 15:3; and see 2 Cor. 3:10–11.
4. Neh. 7:69.
5. Matt. 22:34–40; 23:23.
6. Matt. 5:19.
7. Matt. 5:17–20.
8. John 14:6.
9. John 8:32, 36.
10. Matt. 23:4.

Holy Spirit or Blueprint?

1. 2 Pet. 1:3.
2. The much-needed central thrust of the work of Stanley Hauerwas concerns an "ethic of character." He insists that if we shape the person, not only will the person's behavior change, the very "ethical situation" that person faces will be different. See, for example, his *A Community of Character* (London: University of Notre Dame, 1986) or *Character and the Christian Life* (London: University of Notre Dame, 1994). See, too, Bruce Birch and Larry Rasmussen's *Bible and Ethics in the Christian Life,* rev. ed. (Minneapolis: Augsburg Fortress, 1989). These are not devotional reading.
3. Rom. 12:2 NEB.
4. 2 Cor. 3:18.
5. Lev. 19:9–10.
6. *The Mishnah,* trans. Herbert Danby (Oxford: Oxford University Press, 1987).

7. Read no more than the whole nineteenth chapter of Leviticus to experience the repetition of this phrase, which acts as the basis of response even in areas where there are no specifics.

8. John 7:15.

9. John 7:17–19.

10. John 4:34; 5:30; 6:38; 12:28.

11. John 5:41–47.

12. *The Gospel According to John* (Grand Rapids: Eerdmans, 1979), 406.

Changing Jobs?

1. 1 Cor. 10:31.

2. In Esther 4:14, Mordecai tells reluctant Esther, "And who knows but that you have come to royal position for such a time as this?" Looking back on it, we are able to see what Mordecai couldn't be sure of. Even Acts 16:10 says the group "concluded" that God had called them to Macedonia.

Musings on Truth and Tolerance

1. See Niebuhr's *Social Sources of Denominationalism.*

2. This is too broad an area to enter here, but there's no denying that the existence of hundreds of different fellowships dishonors God, hinders his work, and breaks hearts. More should be done to heal divisions. On the other hand, it makes no sense to claim, as many critics do, that the very existence of various churches is the proof of stupidity and mutual bitterness. This is a complex area, and critics should try to be fair.

3. Gal. 5:4; 1 Tim. 1:19–20; 2 Pet. 2:1; 2 John 7–11.

4. Rom. 3:29–30. See also Acts 10:34–36: "I see quite plainly that God has no favorites, but that he who reverences Him and lives a good life in any nation is welcomed by Him" (Moffatt).

Truth Is for Doing

1. 1 John 3:7.
2. 1 John 1:6 ASV.
3. 1 John 3:17–18.
4. John 13:17.
5. Matt. 7:24, 26.
6. James 1:22–25.
7. 1 Thess. 4:3.
8. *Include Me Out* (London: Epworth Press, 1968), 36. I've leaned heavily on Morris in this piece for both content and phrasing.
9. Amos 5:14–15, 23–24 TEV.

No Dead End!

1. The story is told in Boreham's *The Home of the Echoes* (London: Epworth Press, 1928), 24–35.
2. Isa. 33:17–19; 36–37.
3. John 21:3–14.
4. Luke 24:1–3.
5. John 10.10.

Printed in the United States
By Bookmasters